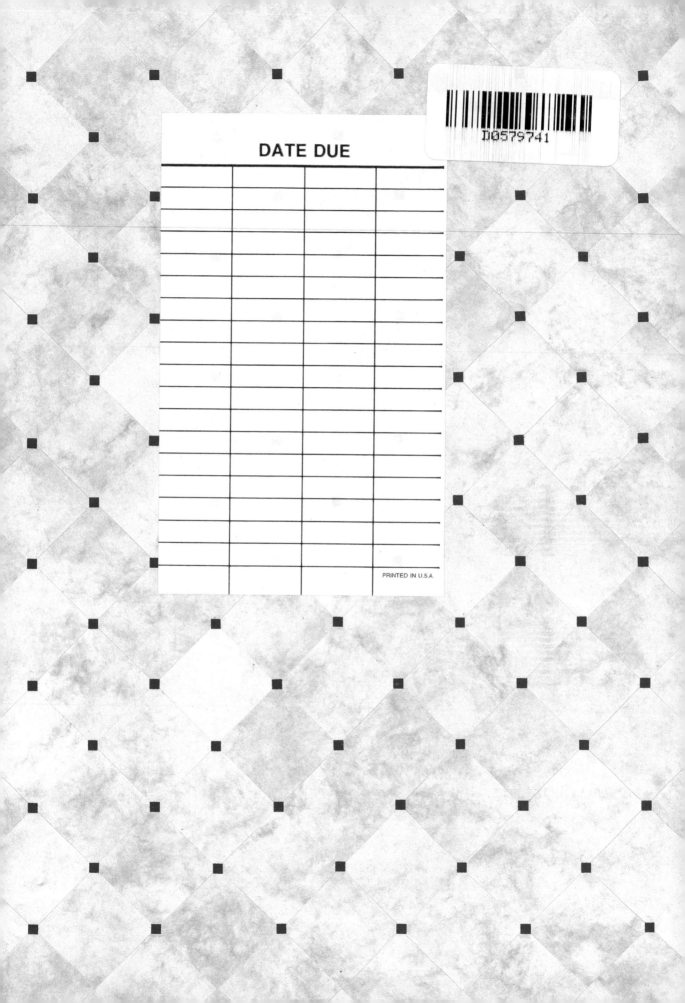

DATE DUE

THE
FLAVORS
OF
ITALY

THE FLAVORS OF ITALY

SIMONETTA LUPI VADA

WITH INTRODUCTORY TEXT BY LINDA SONNTAG

HPBooks®

ANOTHER BEST-SELLING VOLUME FROM HP BOOKS®

Published by HP Books®, P.O. Box 5367, Tuscan, AZ 85703
ISBN: Hardcover 0-89586-521-1
Library of Congress Catalog Card Number: 86-82119

This book was designed and produced by
Quarto Publishing Ltd
The Old Brewery, 6 Blundell Street
London N7 9BH

Senior Editor Tessa Rose
Editors Susie Ward, Lorraine Dickey
Translator Anna Nyburg

Art Editor Nick Clark
Design Penny Dawes
Photographers David Burch, Jon Wyand

Publisher Rick Bailey (HP)
Art Director Alastair Campbell
Executive Editor Randy Summlin (HP)
Editorial Directors Carolyn King, Elaine Woodard (HP)

Typeset by Dimension Ltd, London
Manufactured in Hong Kong by Regent Publishing Services Limited
Printed by Lee Fung Asco Printers Ltd, Hong Kong

CONTENTS

The cooking of Italy is the mother of all European cuisine, a fact acknowledged by even the "Larousse Gastronomique". Its origins are well recorded by the writers of ancient Rome, who have left very vivid impressions of the orgies indulged in by the ruling classes — but this is only half the picture.

THE ORIGINS OF ITALIAN COOKING

For while the aristocracy sat down, or rather reclined, to such dishes as peacock dressed in all its feathers or boar stuffed with live thrushes, the common soldier was roasting his ration of millet on a stone set in the campfire. When it was done, he crushed it, boiled it up with water and ate it as gruel. What was left over solidified into a cake and was consumed cold. This primitive meal was called *pulmentum*, and it has survived right up to the present day in the tastier form of polenta, whereas the more excessive dishes of the Empire, though more memorable, declined and fell with it.

Though what endured was, like polenta, deeply rooted in peasant life, the extravagance of Imperial tables is impossible to ignore. Flamingos and herons were also served up in their plumage; hedgehogs, puppies, wolves and donkeys enjoyed great popularity; dormice were kept in a barrel to stop them losing weight by exercise and were fed until they were fat, then roasted in honey and herbs. A favorite banquet recipe was "Trojan pork". The title referred to the horse of Troy, which had concealed the ambushing Greek soldiers. Trojan pork was stuffed with oysters and songbirds. One side of it was smeared with meal soaked in wine and oil and roasted, then the pig was turned over and the uncooked side was dipped into boiling water until it was done. Among the more exotic delicacies of the day were camel's foot and elephant's trunk.

All these things were consumed in stupendous quantities by the few who could afford them. The Emperor Maximinius is reputed to have eaten over 40 lb of meat a day, and to have drunk 35 pints of wine. The Emperor Aurelian commissioned an actor, Farone, to amuse him by eating in one session a whole sheep, a whole sucking pig and a whole boar, accompanied by 100 buns and 100 bottles of wine.

The ancient Romans were fond of cooking with all the herbs and spices to which their vast empire gave them access. The original Roman seasoning was salt, evapo-

*T*he artist Longlin's depiction of a
sumptuous 18th century banquet, held in
Venice in honor of the visiting Elector of
Cologne.

rated from the water at the mouth of the river Tiber. It was used as a preservative for meat, and when more was made than could be used at home it became the basis for Rome's first important export trade, carried out of the city along the via Salaria — the Salt Road — which remains to this day.

To make salted meat more palatable, the Romans later added honey, dried fruit and spices. The resulting taste was the ancestor of today's agrodolce, a bittersweet sauce enjoyed with many different foods, including game and cabbage. A less attractive flavouring that seems to have been used liberally to disguise the taste of salt meat was *garum,* which one writer described as a sauce made from the entrails of mackerel.

Poultry could be reared by every household and there was a plentiful supply of chickens from Roman markets. Guinea fowl, pigeon and duck were also popular, and when the Romans conquered Gaul they discovered a great liking for goose. Consequently the returning troops drove huge flocks of geese from Picardy to Rome, living off the fields and causing much devastation as they went.

D uring the 2nd century the Emperor Trajan built the Forum, and next to it on Quirinal Hill a supermarket, a semi-circular structure with both open-air and closed booths. Behind it rambled multistorey buildings housing more shops and stalls. There the Romans bought and sold meat and poultry, fish and wine. Olive oil was imported from Spain, wheat from Egypt and spices from Asia.

Cabbage was grown by the better-off, while the poor ate beans, mallow and a species of nettle. Spinach was not known till the 9th century, when it was introduced from Persia. Persia also provided Italy with melons, which farmers began to cultivate at Cantalupo, outside Rome. Figs and wild cherries were highly-prized natives.

Honey was used as a sweetener — even on savoury foods. The Roman dish of honeyed eggs, *ova mellita,* gave its name to today's omelette. Another food given the sweet treatment was cheese. Flour and crushed fresh cheese were mixed with honey and eggs and baked in an earthenware mould — the cheesecake was born. The crushed fresh cheese in question was the ancestor of ricotta, but the Romans had a dozen varieties of cheese, of which they were very fond.

I n the 3rd century AD Rome fell to the barbarians and the excesses of the degenerate empire were replaced by a more sober lifestyle. Recipes were preserved, as were other writings, in monasteries. In the 9th century came the Islamic invasion, which brought a new injection of life into Italian cooking. The Arabs brought with them the techniques of making ice cream and sorbet, and introduced desserts and sweet cakes made with marzipan. They were also responsible for planting the first sugar cane in Europe, but its cultivation did not really catch on until 200 years later, when cane and refined sugar were brought back by the Crusaders. Sugar went under the name of 'Indian salt' and was used as salt was, to season fish and meat. The Crusaders also reintroduced the spices that had been known in the days of ancient Rome, and a new interest in cooking sprang up. Milk and egg pies, vegetable tarts and bread sweetened with dried fruit appeared in a recipe book around 1290, along with the first-ever mention of pasta.

W hen Marco Polo opened up the spice trade between Venice and the Far East, Venetians grew fat on the profits and Venice became a centre of gastronomy. It was there that the table fork became popular and that drinking vessels were first made of fine glass.

In 16th century Florence the first modern cooking academy was set up. Called *Compagnia del Paiolo* (Company of the

Cauldron), one of its members was the painter Andrea del Sarto, who presented his colleagues with an exhibition dish made of gelatine in the shape of a temple held up by pillars of sausages and parmesan. Inside was a book with pages of pasta, and in front stood roasted thrushes, singing notes inscribed on the pasta in peppercorns.

In 1533 Catherine de Medici journeyed from Florence to France to marry the future King Henri II. France was still in the dark ages as far as the art of cooking was concerned, and Catherine took with her her own chefs and pastrycooks, who were adept at making ices, cakes and cream puffs. Marie de Medici followed in her footsteps in 1600 to become the bride of Henri IV. The Florentines were responsible for introducing haricot beans, petit pois, broccoli, artichokes and savoy cabbage to the French, and they also educated them in the culinary skills that were soon to make their own cuisine great and renowned the world over.

F rom Italy too came the double boiler. The French adopted it as the bain marie, but the original Mary's bath or *bagno maria* was named after its inventor Maria de Cleofsa, an alchemist who devised it to help her with her arcane researches into the relationship between magic, medicine and cooking.

The 16th century saw the arrival of the first tomato in Italy, brought back to Europe with the first red pepper from Mexico by the Spanish conquistadors. Called the *pomo d'oro* (golden apple), it was a cherry-sized yellow fruit used as a salad vegetable. It took 200 years for the large luscious red varieties to be developed for use in cooking.

Coffee was imported from the East. In 1585 Venice's ambassador to Turkey described to the Senate "the habit of the Turks of drinking a black water as hot as you can bear it, taken from seeds called *cavee*, and they say it has the power of keeping men awake". Its popularity was quickly established in Venice and soon spread all over Europe.

The arrival of the potato was greeted with less enthusiasm. Pope Clement VII's botanist classified the specimen presented to him as "a small truffle" and thenceforward it was cultivated in Italian gardens — as a decorative plant. The Italians were not alone in their confusion as to what to do with the potato — Queen Elizabeth I's chef threw away the tubers and served up the leaves. Potatoes never became a staple in Italy, even when their true use was discovered. Corn, the last major import, which came from America, provided a more popular alternative form of starch.

B y the 16th century the French had become so advanced in the art of cooking that chefs from the French court were sent back to Venice to demonstrate their skills. The Venetians were not impressed. "French cooks have ruined the Venetian stomach," wrote Gerolamo Zanetti, "with so much porcherie (filth)... sauces, broths, extracts... garlic and onion in every dish... meat and fish transformed to such a point that they are scarcely recognizable by the time they get to the table... Everything mashed and mixed up with a hundred herbs, spices, sauces..."

Though the author was a biased (Venetian) observer writing some 400 years ago, his comment serves to underline the major difference between present-day Italian and French cooking. For while French cuisine tends to be elaborate and subtle, that of Italy is bold, simple and direct. Zanetti's mistrust of foreigners' meddling with good basic ingredients, transforming them into something "scarcely recognizable", also shows a fierce respect for local tradition that is very much part of Italian cooking today. It is not just influence from abroad that is resisted, but influence from other regions of Italy, and it is this that makes Italian cooking so varied and so unique.

Italian cooking is the cooking of its regions. Until 1861 the regions of Italy were separate and often hostile states. Geographically as well as politically isolated from each other, the regions developed their own entirely distinctive culinary character and traditions, traditions that are fiercely and proudly preserved today.

In Italy what is local is best. An Emilian would regard a salami produced in neighboring Tuscany with scepticism; a Tuscan might smile ruefully at the Emilian's extravagant use of butter and cream. It follows that the traveler intent on enjoying Italian food should always order what the locals eat. It is no good asking for osso buco in Naples or beefsteak in Genoa, because they will be but pale imitations of the genuine things to be had in Milan and Florence — and you will have missed the opportunity to sample the perfect spaghetti alla marinara and torta pasqualina.

Italian pride in local fare and disdain of "imports," be they from only a few miles away, is soundly rooted in a love of fresh food. If there is one aspect of cooking shared by all the regions of Italy, it is the importance placed on the quality of the ingredients. Fruit and vegetables must be home-grown, preferably without chemical fertilizers, and picked at the peak of ripeness and glossy perfection. A squeeze of lemon juice is known to have more zest when the lemon

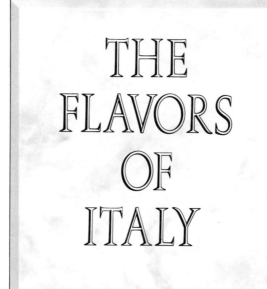

THE FLAVORS OF ITALY

is freshly picked from the tree and still warm from the sun, than when it has traveled long distances, ripening slowly in a crate. Meat should be home-reared and home-killed, and fish straight from the catch — seafood is rarely served at any distance from the coast.

All over Italy, Italians treat their food with respect. Their cooking is designed to emphasize the natural flavors of the ingredients. In this it is very different from French cooking, with its subtle harmonies and sophisticated sauces. Italian food is brightly colored in the market place, and just as brightly colored when it reappears on the plate. It is good, wholesome, hearty and endlessly varied — essentially home cooking that requires very few special skills to master.

The main meal in Italy is eaten in the middle of the day and can consist of several courses. First there may be a soup. This is usually a clear broth made substantial with rice or pasta, shredded vegetables or the dumplings made of potato or semolina called gnocchi. An alternative to soup would

*T*he foodshops of Bologna, which is renowned as the gastronomic capital of Italy, are Aladdin's caves for the gourmet. A dazzling display of sausages, cheeses, mushrooms, preserved fruits and pickled vegetables compete for the shopper's attention.

be a risotto or a dish of baked or boiled pasta with a piquant or creamy sauce. Generous helpings of freshly grated parmesan cheese top this first course. Next comes a dish of fish or meat. In some areas the meat would be quite plainly cooked, perhaps broiled with aromatic olive oil and herbs as its only added flavoring; in others it might be a more complicated dish layered with melting cheese and tender ham, coated in breadcrumbs and fried in pork fat until succulent and golden.

A *contorno* — literally a contour — of seasonal vegetables or salad can be served with or after this course. To finish with, there will be fruit and local cheese, and the meal is of course accompanied by the wine of the region.

On Sundays or special occasions lunch may begin with antipasti — a selection of salami, fish, olives, artichokes and other savory appetizers both hot and cold — and end with one Italy's famous desserts, ices, cakes or pastries and black espresso coffee and liqueurs.

Lazio, Umbria and the Marches

This central band across the knee of Italy is dominated by the capital, Rome. The Roman appetite is robust and hearty, and the food that satisfies it is both good and simple. Suckling pig stuffed with herbs and roasted on a spit is a typical favorite dish. The Roman gastronomic calendar moves from festival to festival, with roast capon at Christmas, stuffed with breadcrumbs, salami, giblets and cheese; suckling lamb at Easter, and on Midsummer Night, snails in a sauce of garlic, anchovy, tomato and mint.

In Rome you can eat both the fresh home-made pasta of the north, in a justly famous dish of cannelloni — flat pasta sheets rolled around a meat filling — and the dried tubular

THE REGIONS OF ITALY

The regions listed below represent the main geographical divisions of Italy. The shields shown are those of the main town or city in each region. Each recipe is accompanied by one of these shields to denote its known, or suspected, origin.

KEY TO REGIONS

LAZIO, UMBRIA AND THE MARCHES
(See below left)

TUSCANY
(See p.16)

EMILIA-ROMAGNA
(See p.18)

LIGURIA
(See p.20)

VENETO
(See p.21)

LOMBARDY
(See p.23)

PIEDMONT
(See p.26)

SICILY
(See p.29)

NAPLES AND THE SOUTH: CAMPANIA, CALABRIA, BASILICATA, APULIA AND ABRUZZI-MOLISE
(See p.26)

SARDINIA
(See p.29)

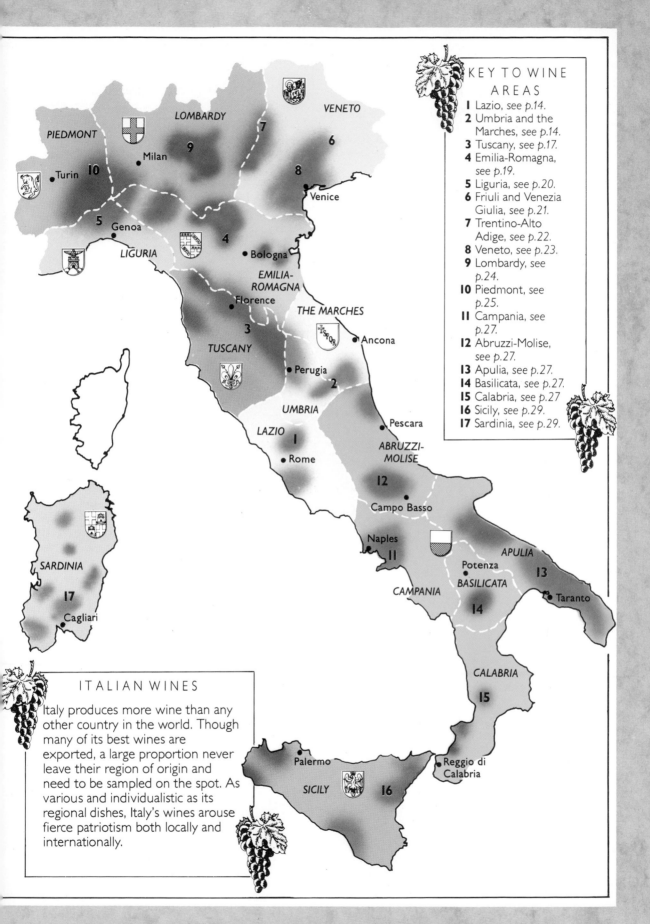

KEY TO WINE
AREAS

1 Lazio, see p.14.
2 Umbria and the
  Marches, see p.14.
3 Tuscany, see p.17.
4 Emilia-Romagna,
  see p.19.
5 Liguria, see p.20.
6 Friuli and Venezia
  Giulia, see p.21.
7 Trentino-Alto
  Adige, see p.22.
8 Veneto, see p.23.
9 Lombardy, see
  p.24.
10 Piedmont, see
   p.25.
11 Campania, see
   p.27.
12 Abruzzi-Molise,
   see p.27.
13 Apulia, see p.27.
14 Basilicata, see p.27.
15 Calabria, see p.27
16 Sicily, see p.29.
17 Sardinia, see p.29.

ITALIAN WINES

Italy produces more wine than any
other country in the world. Though
many of its best wines are
exported, a large proportion never
leave their region of origin and
need to be sampled on the spot. As
various and individualistic as its
regional dishes, Italy's wines arouse
fierce patriotism both locally and
internationally.

THE WINES OF LAZIO, UMBRIA AND THE MARCHES

LAZIO

Lazio has two main wine-producing areas: the Castelli Romani in the hills around Rome and the area around Lake Bolsena, about 60 miles from it.

CASTELLI ROMANI

This is an area of 50 sq miles in the Alban hills producing mainly white wine that can be either sweet or dry. The grapes for the sweet wine are allowed to dry out a little on the vine before they are picked and fermented in the caves of the Alban hills. The sweet wines go well with fresh fruit and the dry complement robust Roman pasta dishes and their suckling pigs and baby lambs. The best known of these wines is Frascati, clear gold in color and either dry, semi-sweet or sweet.

CASTELBRACCIANO

A sweet, golden-yellow wine from the shores of Lake Bracciano.

CASTRENSE

Light red and white wines from the shores of Lake Bolsena.

CECUBO

A wine from Gaeta drunk by Cicero and Horace. It is a very light red with a full fragrance.

EST! EST!! EST!!!

There is a curious tale of how this wine came by its name. Local legend has it that an 18th century cardinal on a journey around Italy sent his steward before him to try out the wines in various hostelries. When the steward discovered a good one, he was to chalk *Est!* ("It is") on the door. At Montefiascone he was so impressed that he chalked *Est! Est!! Est!!!* before passing out into a stupor. The cardinal arrived and his enthusiasm for the wine was so great that he drank himself to death on it there and then.

UMBRIA AND THE MARCHES

Wine production here is not extensive. The hillsides are very steep and in many cases vines are grown alternating with rows of corn. Both red and white are generally on the rough side, but there are two notable exceptions — Verdicchio dei Castelli di Jesi from the Marches, and Orvieto from Umbria.

ALTE VALLE DEL TENERE

The wines of the upper Tiber, both red and white, are light and simple and ideal for lunchtime drinking.

BIANCHELLO

A light dry white from the Marches, it goes well with fish.

ORVIETO

Made mainly from the Trebbiano grape, this wine has been produced around the cathedral city of Orvieto for at least 500 years. There are two straw-colored whites, one dry and the other semi-sweet. The grapes for the semi-sweet are allowed to begin to rot after they have been picked — in the German Auslese the grapes start to rot on the vine — and the resulting wine is not too sweet to be drunk with fish or poultry. The dry Orvieto is the more popular export.

VERDICCHIO DEI CASTELLI DI JESI

This wine is drunk along the holiday coast around Rimini and is also exported in large quantities. It is one of the very best of the Italian whites, despite the vulgar bottle. Straw-colored and slightly bitter, the best Verdicchio has a secondary fermentation like Chianti.

VINCOTTO

"Cooked wine" is made by reducing must over heat and then topping it up with uncooked must. The wine is fermented and kept for two years. It is strong, rich and sweet.

The Italians' passion for ice cream dates back to the days of the Roman empire, when snow and crushed berries were served at the imperial table.

pasta of the south. Sauces include tuna and mushrooms (alla carrettiera), hot red peppers (all'arrabbiata — rabid!) and the celebrated *alla carbonara*, made with salt pork, eggs and cream.

Saltimbocca, the picturesque name meaning "jump in the mouth", is slices of ham atop slices of veal, flavored with sage, fried in butter and then braised in white wine. Straciatella is another well-known dish, a clear soup with a mixture of eggs, flour and cheese poured into it. It breaks up as it cooks, forming the "little rags" that give the soup its name.

For dessert you might be offered zuppa inglese, neither soup nor English, but a rich trifle flavored with rum.

The mountainous region of Umbria is the biggest producer — and hence consumer — of meat in the whole of Italy. There is plenty of game in the higher regions, sheep and goats a little further down and cattle and pigs on the foothills. The pork in particular is

excellent. The animals are fattened on acorns and much of the meat is cured and turned into sausages spiced with garlic, pepper, pine nuts and fennel.

Umbria is famed even in France for its superb truffles, eaten sliced on pasta, and for its freshwater fish, in particular the roach. The capital of Umbria is Perugia, which is reckoned to manufacture the best chocolates in the world.

Most of the inhabitants of the Marches live along the coast, and it follows that fish is the staple of their diet. Each seaside town has its own way of making fish soup, with the ingredients varying according to the day's catch. Snails flavored with fennel, and huge fat olives — stuffed, rolled in breadcrumbs and fried — are other delicacies to be had in the region, while Urbino in the north is distinguished by its sauce. It was first invented by a Duke of Urbino in the 15th century, who was so afraid of being poisoned that he refused to let his chef season his food. Once the food had been tasted for him he added his own sauce, prepared according to a secret recipe by a sevant whom he trusted.

The recipe was recently rediscovered and the sauce is produced today in a bottle with the Duke's portrait on the label. His profile is disfigured by the removal of the bridge of his nose — a piece of self-inflicted surgery. The Duke's right eye was blinded by the claws of a falcon, and he had the top of his nose cut away so that he could see with his left eye if a would-be assassin was attempting to sneak up on him from the right.

Tuscany

T uscany is the heart of Italy. Its food is simply prepared and with the best ingredients. Elaborate dishes have no place on the menu here; indeed the Tuscan way of cooking is sometimes looked upon by outsiders as austere because of its conspicuous lack of complicated sauces and seasonings.

Florence is the capital and, in culinary terms, Florentine (alla fiorentina) is synonymous with spinach. But this is only outside Italy — to an Italian *alla fiorentina* simply means "in the Florentine style." Bistecca alla fiorentina is a typical Tuscan dish well worth traveling miles to sample in its native city — it is simply prepared with ingredients of the highest quality, and it does not contain spinnach. Bistecca alla fiorentina is steak from a choice two-year-old Chiana Valley bull, broiled briefly above chestnut wood. It is salted and rubbed with a little olive oil just before it is removed from the fire and served perhaps with fresh beans.

Tuscans are known throughout Italy as mangiafagioli (bean eaters). They eat beans in soup, beans in risotto and beans with pasta. Beans and tuna fish is a favorite appetizer. Fagioli nel fiasco is beans cooked slowly in a closed flask to prevent the flavor from escaping. They are then eaten simply with

*P*esaro, like all Italian coastal towns, has its own recipe for fish soup, the ingredients for which vary from day to day according to the fishermen's catch.

THE WINES OF TUSCANY

The landscape of Tuscany used to reflect the diet of its inhabitants: bread, olive oil and wine. Corn, olive trees and vines would be grown in the same field, with perhaps a cow or two wandering among them. The peasants had to give half their produce to the landowners and could not risk a single crop. Now the vines have taken over in rows well-spaced enough to allow the passage of a tractor. Still, a few farmers have kept their olive trees, as much because the grey-green colour is a vital part of the landscape as for their oil.

ARBIA

A dry white wine that goes well with the pecorino — sheep's cheese — of the region. A "virgin" wine, because the must is fermented without stalks or skin.

BRUNELLO DI MONTALCINO

One of the great Italian reds — full and fragrant, smooth and well balanced, it is aged in the cask for five or six years and enthusiasts recommend keeping it in the bottle for up to 50.

CANDIA

Sweet red and white wines from the northwest of the region.

CHIANTI

Baron Bettino Ricasoli "invented" Chianti in the 1860s. When his young wife danced at a ball with a man who seemed to be paying her too much attention, he called her away and they drove all night to Brolio, where there was a gloomy castle the baron's family had not lived in for years. Here they set up a permanent home well away from the temptations of society. The baron diverted himself by developing a new wine — a mixture of black Sangiovese and white Malvasia grapes, and a method of making them ferment twice, giving the wine a novel taste a slight tingle. When the first fermentation is over, a rich must from dried grapes is added to the wine, inducing a second fermentation that lasts from two to three weeks. Wines made by this method are drunk young and sold in typical Chianti flasks covered in wicker (or plastic). Finer Chiantis meant to be aged are only fermented once and sold in ordinary claret bottles. Chainti is produced and exported on a very large scale, but Chianti classico comes only from the area between Florence and Siena and bears the growers' label of a black cockerel against a gold background.

MOSCADELLO DI MONTALCINO

A light, golden, fragrant wine with a slight tingle, drunk young and chilled.

UGOLINO BIANCO

A clear straw-colored white from near Livorno. To be drunk young and chilled with fish.

VAL DI CHIANA

A clear, golden-yellow wine, a "virgin" like Arbia, see above left.

VERNACCIA DI SAN GIMIGNANO

A fresh, straw-colored wine with a hint of bitterness comes from around this picturesque town, which has been completely overtaken by tourism. It is a fine, dry white that improves with age.

VIN NOBILE DI MONTEPULCIANO

A smooth, well-balanced ruby red wine with a hint of violet, best after at least five years in the bottle.

VIN SANTO

A rich, sweet dessert wine, very popular in Tuscany.

*T*he Ponte Vecchio in Florence, the city
whose chefs and pastry cooks were
responsible for educating the French in
the culinary arts.

olive oil, salt, pepper and lemon juice and a loaf of flat Tuscan bread.

The bread in Tuscany is unsalted, as it forms a component part of so many dishes that a too-salty flavor would ruin. There is, for example, a bread salad, tossed with tomatoes, cucumber and pink onions, and a bread and tomato soup, especially beloved by children. The other reason that bread is not salted is that salt absorbs moisture, and bread is bought in big enough quantities to last a week. Salted bread would go moldy before the week was out. The Tuscans are a practical and economy-conscious people.

They are very fond of game, particularly pheasant and hare, which is plentiful in the hillsides, and which they serve simply roasted and flavored with wild rosemary. Their pecorino cheese with its sharp flavor and black crust is one of the best in Italy and is an excellent accompaniment to Chianti,

Tuscany's famous wine.

There are two more specialties of the region that deserve a mention — Livorno's splendid fish soup, cacciucco alla livornese, and Siena's flat dessert cake, panforte, full of dried fruit, almonds and spices, often taken home by tourists as a souvenir of the lovely medieval city that makes it.

Emilia-Romagna

This rich and fertile region lying to the north of Tuscany is Italy's land of plenty, and not for nothing is its capital, Bologna, known as *Bologna la grassa* — "the fat." Bologna is the home of mortadella, perhaps Italy's finest sausage, and, above all, fresh pasta. Made from local wheat milled very fine, bolognese pasta is rolled out so thinly you can almost see through it, cut into long narrow strips to make tagliatelle and served with a tasty ragu, which comes from the French word ragoût, or stew. It is said that the inventor of tagliatelle was inspired by the fine flaxen hair of Lucretia Borgia and that the inventor of tortellini, little stuffed rings of pasta, fell in love with his employer's wife when he saw her sleeping in the nude and promptly produced a new pasta in the shape of her navel.

Tortellini stuffed with turkey, sausage, ham, pork, egg and cheese are traditionally served on Christmas Day as a first course with a rich sauce of butter and cream and topped with grated cheese. Lasagne, baked in the oven with layers of meat and cream sauces, and cappelletti, "little hats," stuffed with ricotta, chicken, egg and spices, are other popular forms of pasta in Bologna.

Emilians are very fond of veal and serve it in their typically extravagant way, stuffed with cheese and ham and braised in wine, a habit that would horrify their plainer-living Tuscan neighbors.

In Emilia is the city of Parma, renowned throughout the world for its prosciutto or Parma ham, and for having given its name to parmesan cheese. The original Parmesan is made in Reggio nell'Emilia and is known variously as parmigiano reggiano or formaggio di grana, "grained cheese," because of its finely-grained texture.

From Modena comes zampone, stuffed foreleg of pork, and from Piacenza *bomba*

THE WINES OF EMILIA-ROMAGNA

The wines of this region are not as full and flavorsome as its cooking. Its most famous wine is Lambrusco, a dry sparkling red, beloved by the Bolognese and arousing strong reactions in visitors from outside the region, who are either captivated or repelled.

ALBANA

A well-balanced, yellow-gold wine grown around the town of Bertinoro.

Light and fresh with a slight sweetness, but nevertheless delicious with fish.

CASTELFRANCO

A fragrant dry white wine from around Modena, made from

a mixture of grapes grown in the same vineyard.

GUTTURNIO

A dryish, ruby-red wine, best drunk very young and

served cool, made mainly from Barbera grapes.

LAMBRUSCO

Dry, red and sparkling, very pink and frothy when poured, but the bubbles subside to a tingle. The Bolognese

say that its fresh, clean taste complements their rich cooking and that it aids the digestion.

SANGIOVESE

A fresh, ruby-red wine with a hint of garnet, widely grown throughout the

region. Fruity when young, it mellows with age and is well prized by the locals.

SCANDIANO BIANCO

A popular, straw-yellow wine, this is not renowned for its quality outside the

region. There are still dry and sparkling sweet varieties.

TREBBIANO

This grape is widely grown in the region, producing wines of different style and quality. The more common variety is drunk young, but

there is also a sharp elegant wine that goes well with fish and a sweeter, sparkling Trebbiano for dessert.

THE WINES OF LIGURIA

Liguria is a small region and an even smaller wine producer, with most of the vineyards growing enough to supply only their owners' tables. Genoa is the center of the Italian wine trade, but it deals in the wines of the rest of Italy and drinks its own at home.

BARBAROSSA

So called because of the way the grape grows in "red beards".

A festive pink wine, there is also a sweet variety.

CAMPOCHIESA BIANCO

A full-flavored dry white wine from the Pigato grape, Campochiesa improves with age.

Traditionally it is laid down at the birth of a son to be drunk at his wedding.

CINQUETERRE

Drunk young, this is a delicate, clear, yellow-gold wine with a slightly bitter taste, made from the Vernaccia grape. It comes from five villages — hence its name — high up in

rocky terrain. There is a sweet variety made from grapes part-dried in the sun. It has a high alcohol content (16%) and is much enjoyed with ice cream.

CORONATA

A dry white wine with a sharp fresh

taste that goes very well with fish.

DOLCEACQUA

Made mainly from Rosesse grapes, this is a full, heavy, aromatic wine that goes well

with stronger-flavored local dishes, such as pesto.

di riso, a pudding-shaped mold of rice cooked in white wine that contains vegetables and pigeons cooked in red wine. In Ferrara the local delicacy is broiled eel and at Ravenna you can sample another Italian fish soup, *brodetto.*

Liguria

T his is the narrow strip of coast that stretches from San Remo to La Spezia and is bordered to the north by the Alps and Apennines. Its capital is the great port of Genoa and its culinary traditions, not surprisingly, reflect the seafaring nature of its inhabitants. For the fishermen who spent weeks at sea, food had to be prepared to keep. Lentils, garbanzo beans and dried beans, pies and savory cookies were eaten at sea and when they returned home, the sailors satisfied their cravings for fresh green vegetables with tarts filled with artichokes, spinach, zucchini, Swiss chard and wild herbs — torta pasqualina. Genoa's favorite herb is basil, the main ingredient for pesto sauce. The word comes from "pestle." Basil, garlic, parmesan, olive oil and pine nuts — and sometimes lemon peel, beans and potatoes — are pounded together with a pestle in a mortar and served with gnocchi or pasta.

The land of Liguria is not good farming land, so every little bit of vegetation must be put to good use. One recipe calls for wild herbs, "the kind you find growing on the garden wall." The Ligurian frugality was responsible for the invention of ravioli — the word comes from robiole, or leftovers — little scraps stuffed into envelopes of pasta. *Cappon magro* is a true Genoese joke. Literally "thin capon," it is a dish that contains no meat at all. It is, for all that, a very majestic concoction and has been pronounced worthy of Homeric heroes. Layered boiled vegetables and pickled fish are built up to form a huge colorful

Venice is a city of exotic culinary contrasts, a legacy from its position at the center of the spice trade in the middle ages. Here, some of the finest restaurants in Europe pay as much attention to the preparation of Risi e Bisi, a simple dish of rice and peas, as they do to scampi, oysters and caviar. Risi e Bisi was, after all, the favorite dish of the doges.

dome which is then draped in a green sauce flavored with herbs.

Veneto

Veneto, with Trentino to the west and Friuli-Venezia Guilia to the east, is one of Italy's major wine producing areas and its famous exports include Soave, Valpolicella and Bardolino. Its gastronomic center is its capital, Venice, whose cuisine still reflects the legacy of the medieval spice trade. Here you can enjoy lightly curried fish and a delicate dish of peppered calf's liver and onions. The Venetians' taste is, on the whole, exotic. They like rice with jumbo shrimp, squid or shrimp in a garlic and tomato sauce, and even rice with grapes, cheese and garlic. Salt cod is cooked with cinnamon, turkey with pomegranate sauce and zucchini flowers are fried in butter.

Pasta is not much eaten in Veneto. Instead the locals favor polenta, which is not yellow

THE WINES OF FRIULI-VENEZIA GIULIA

The character of this region is more Slavic than Italian and the inhabitants are less patriotic than anywhere else in Italy. You are quite as likely to be served a Yugoslavian wine or a wine from Veneto as one grown locally.

GAMAY

A brilliant ruby-red wine from vines imported from France. Gamay grows well on the hills of the region and has a faint strawberry taste when young.

PICCOLIT

A golden-yellow dessert wine drunk chilled. It was much admired in European courts at the turn of the century and is best when it has aged a few years in the bottle. Piccolit grapes are part-dried in the sun after being picked to give the wine a more concentrated sweetness.

PINOT GRIGIO

Arguably the best white wine of the region, it has a slightly pink tinge and a faint tang of nutmeg. There are also smooth red and spumante versions.

SAUVIGNON

Another grape imported from France and grown widely throughout the region. An elegant, straw-yellow wine with a slightly bitter aftertaste.

TOCAI

A dry yellow-white wine quite unlike the Hungarian Tokay, which is a great dessert wine. Makes a very good accompaniment to fish dishes.

Lombardy is a region of dairy farms and rice production. It is famous for gorgonzola and bel paese cheeses and for its tradition of long, slow cooking, which survives not only in small hilltop towns like this one but also in the region's capital, Milan.

THE WINES OF TRENTINO — ALTO ADIGE

Alto Adige, which its inhabitants call the South Tyrol, is German-speaking, and the wines have German names and are exported to Germany, Switzerland and Austria. The wines are finer and quite distinct from those produced in Trentino, which are less numerous.

BLAUBURGUNDER

A reliable, full red wine from the Pinot noir grape grown around Bolzano, Caldaro and Terlano.

CALDARO

Lago di Caldaro is a full red wine with a slight almond flavor. Often called Kalterersee, the German name for the lake.

COLLINE BOLZANO

Red wines from the Schiavone grapes grown on the hills around Bolzano. Variable in quality.

GEWÜRZTRAMINER

In the South Tyrol is the village of Tramin, or Termeno, which the locals claim gave Gewürztraminer its name. But the white wine from this region is not as full or fragrant as its more famous namesake from Alsace.

RIESLING

A well-balanced wine, the Terlaner Riesling is one of the few whites of the area that are exported.

SANTA MAGDALENA

The finest red wine of this region — a brilliant ruby with a hint of orange, it is smooth with a slightly bitter aftertaste. Made from Schiava and Schiavone grapes, grown in the hills east of Bolzano.

THE WINES OF VENETO

One of the major wine-growing regions, Veneto produces Valpolicella, Bardolino and Soave, three of Italy's best known exports.

BARDOLINO

A bright, ruby-red wine with a fresh taste, made from a variety of grapes grown on the eastern shores of Lake Garda. Best drunk young and cool.

CABERNET

A full-bodied, vigorous red with a slight amber tint, best after it has spent at least three years in the bottle. It has woodland flavors of raspberry and honey with a hint of violet.

COLLI DI VALDOBBIADENE

A dry white with a hint of bitterness, and a sweet, slightly sparkling dessert wine, both bear this name.

MERLOT

A ruby-red wine with a fresh taste and a hint of almond. The Merlot grape is grown all over Italy; the Veneto Merlot is lighter than that from Trentino.

PROSECCO

A straw-yellow wine, aromatic and fresh. There is also a sparkling variety — Prosecco Spumante. Prosecco is grown all over the north of Italy.

RABOSO

A rather rough red wine common across the region, and best drunk young.

RECIOTO

A red wine so-called because it is made only from the "ears" (*orecchie*) of the bunches of grapes, which are riper than the rest. It is full and heavy and makes a good accompaniment to roast meat and mature cheese. A sweet sparkling variety can be drunk with dessert.

SOAVE

Smooth, dry and straw-yellow, this is one of the finest Italian whites. It is made mainly from Garganega grapes and is best drunk young and chilled as an accompaniment to the fish dishes of Venice.

VALPOLICELLA

Slightly fuller than Bardolino, this is the most popular red of the region. It can be aged in the bottle, but is perhaps best drunk cool and young.

as in most other parts of Italy, but white, made from the fine white corn grown in Friuli-Giulia. Another simple dish prized by the Venetians is *risi e bisi,* rice and peas. This falls somewhere between a soup and a risotto and is made at its best with the tender young peas available only in spring.

The merchants of Venice first introduced sugar into Europe and Venetians today still have a sweet tooth. In the middle of the morning the city is full of people sitting under awnings enjoying their *ombrina* — "little shade" — a glass of wine or a cup of coffee and sweet cornmeal cookies or the vanilla cake called pandoro.

Lombardy

L ombardy's national dish is risotto alla milanese, rice delicately flavored and colored with saffron. Another specialty is osso buco, braised veal shank on the bone, of which the marrow is considered to be the tastiest part. To the Milanese goes the credit of inventing another famous meat dish, the Wiener Schnitzel. The original costoletta alla milanese, the breaded veal chop, was taken back to Vienna in the 19th century by General Radetzky, and the Viennese promptly adopted them as their own.

Milan is Italy's financial capital and though

the pace of life there is fast, cooking methods are traditionally slow and housewives spend long hours at the stove, braising, stewing, spit-roasting and gently simmering meat to succulent perfection. It is generally held in France that the Italians overcook their meat, and certainly they like it well done.

Though Lombardy is famous for its rice, it does not grow quite so much of it as Piedmont. It is primarily an area of wheat and dairy farming. Butter is the cooking medium and there are some excellent cheeses, among them gorgonzola. In Milan is the Via dei Ghiottoni, the street of gourmets (or gluttons), which is lined with food shops of every possible sort. One in particular, called Peck, is internationally renowned for its enormous selection of cheeses and its top-quality veal and cured meats. One of the more unusual of these is bresaola, beef salted and dried and sliced paper-thin to be eaten with olive oil, lemon juice and pepper.

Every visitor to Milan is sure to be offered a slice of panettone, a leavened cake made with eggs, raisins and candied peel that is the ideal breakfast accompaniment to a cup of coffee. Torrone is an almond-flavored dessert cake that has been a popular treat since

THE WINES OF LOMBARDY

In the Valtelline, with the Alps to the north and the mountains of Bergamo to the south, the aristocratic Nebbiolo produces fine red wines as in Piedmont — Sassella, Grumello and Inferno. But they are quite elusive and inconsistent in quality and are often exported to Switzerland or appear under a brand name. The other main wine-producing areas are around Lake Garda and to the south of the Po in the Oltrepo Pavese.

CHIARETTO DEL GARDA

The red wines around Lake Garda are very light, and the rosés darker than the French ones. This is an intense pink wine made from a mixture of four types of grape. It has a sharp fresh taste and should be drunk young and cool. A good wine to choose for an outdoor lunch.

COLLINE DEL GARDA AND COLLINE MANTOVANE

Red, white and rosé wines from the area between Lake Garda and Mantua. The reds are very light and clear and all should be drunk young and cool.

FRANCIACORTA

A brilliant ruby-red wine with a fresh taste and a hint of raspberry.

FRECCIAROSSA

Frecciarossa is a village in the Oltrepo Pavese where the Odero family produce four fine wines bottled on their estate in the French style. Each has a brand name: the dry white is called "La Vigne Blanche," the medium dry white "Sillery," the rosé "Saint George" and the red, considered one of the finest Italian reds, is named "Le Grand Cru."

LACRIMA VITIS

A golden dessert wine made from Moscato grapes, partly dried in the sun after picking.

LUGANA

A fresh, dry white made from Trebbiano grapes and aged in the cask before bottling. It has a pale golden color and a slight saffron taste which goes very well with fish.

VALTELLINE REDS

Sassella, Grumello and Inferno are the great red wines of Lombardy, grown in terraces along the River Adda, which flows into Lake Como. They are made from 85 per cent of Nebbiolo grapes and benefit from aging in the bottle. Drink them with broiled and roast meat and game.

THE WINES OF PIEDMONT

Fine wines have been grown in Piedmont since Roman times. The vineyards are gently sloping, the sun is not too fierce, and the vines are protected from the wind by the Alps. Most of the region's wine is full-bodied red, but it also produces the sparkling white Asti Spumante. Turin is the centre of vermouth production, which mostly uses the cheaper wine of Apulia. The vermouth's aroma comes from the herbs in the mountains nearby.

ASTI SPUMANTE

A sparkling, sweet white wine made from the Moscato grape, which is widely grown in Piedmont, Asti is made by the *cuve close* method — fermented in closed vats and bottled under pressure. This is quicker and cheaper than the *méthode champagnoise*, which involves secondary fermentation in the bottle, and which is also used in this region to produce some sparkling dry whites, for example Gancia Royal Cuvée. Asti is a classic dessert wine that can also be enjoyed mid-morning or at parties.

BARBARESCO

A full-bodied, deep red wine made from the Nebbiolo grape, it matures early, taking on a slight amber tint. It comes from the hilly country near Alba.

BARBERA

Piedmont's commonest wine, this is a red that varies greatly in quality. It can be slightly sparkling and sweet; it can be coarse when young or mellow with age. The best Barbera, from around Asti, is granted a growers' association label of blue grapes on the city's red tower.

BAROLO

One of Italy's great wines, Barolo is deep red when young and takes on an amber tinge with age. It is made from the Nebbiolo grape grown in the hills around Alba and is full and fragrant with a hint of violets. Barolo is particularly enjoyable with snails, game and mature cheese.

CORTESE DELL'ALTO MONFERRATO

A light, dry white to be drunk young with fish. A semi-sweet sparkling version is called Cortese di Gavi.

FREISA

A smooth, dry, garnet-red wine from around Turin. It has a hint of raspberries and violets.

GATTINARA

A highly prized garnet-red wine with a hint of raspberries, Gattinara is preferred to Barolo by some connoisseurs. Made from the aristocratic Nebbiolo grape, it is best after three years in the bottle.

GRIGNOLINO D'ASTI

Rose-colored and perfumed, from the Grignolino grape, this is a wine to be drunk young and cool with pasta or poultry.

MOSCATO D'ASTI

A cheaper, commoner version of Asti Spumante.

PASSITO DI CALUSO

A golden-yellow dessert wine, full, round and fruity, made from Erbulace grapes that have been partly dried in the sun after picking to concentrate their sweetness. Excellent with fresh white cheese.

the 13th century, and another favorite Lombardy dessert is pears stuffed with gorgonzola cheese.

Piedmont

Piedmont is a mainly mountainous region and, as in other places with similar terrains, its diet is substantial and sustaining. But its capital, Turin, also has a tradition of culinary sophistication inherited from its great ruling House of Savoy, and this gives Piedmontese cooking an edge of distinction lacking in other mountain areas. Side by side with robust dishes of lasagne, polenta, gnocchi and boiled mixed meats are delicacies such as trout baked on a bed of mushrooms, and bagna cauda, a hot sauce of olive oil, butter, garlic and pounded anchovies, eaten as a dip for cold vegetables, among which is the cardoon, or edible thistle.

Another speciality is fonduta, a kind of fondue made with fat fontina cheese, cornflour, milk and egg yolks, which is sometimes served poured over a slab of polenta and decorated with finely sliced truffles.

The frogs that breed in the rice fields are served up, appropriately, in risotto, and every meal is accompanied by grissini, the long crisp bread sticks that have become synonymous with Italian eating throughout the world. For dessert you might be offered a rich confection of chestnuts and cream called monte bianco, and after the meal a glass of grappa.

Naples and the south

Naples is the gastronomic center of the south, just as Bologna is of the north, and it sets the tone of the cooking of Calabria, Basilicata, Apulia and Abruzzi-Molise, as well as its own region of Campania. Campania is the south's most fertile region and grows wheat, corn and millet as well as huge crops of all kinds of vegetables, especially tomatoes. All the ingredients are to hand for Naples' most celebrated and most exported dish, pizza. In Naples seafood is plentiful and a favorite spaghetti sauce is con vongole, with clams. Campania breeds the large white buffaloes whose milk is turned into mozzarella.

Macugnaga in Piedmont, Italy's prime rice-producing region. The hills here abound in goats and wild boar, and the woods yield up white truffles, which are prized even in France.

THE WINES OF NAPLES AND THE SOUTH

CAMPANIA

Wine has been cultivated here since Roman times, but Campania is not a region renowned for its fine wines. Much of what it produces today is for blending, and a great deal of it, of course, supplies the local tourist trade.

AGLIANICO

A robust red from the grape of the same name, which is grown all over southern Italy.

CAPRI

Red, white and rosé wines come from the island, but there are also mainland wines bottled under the same name. The white is a straw-yellow with a fresh taste and a hint of bitterness and highly thought of by the locals. All three are acceptable table wines made from a mixture of grapes.

COLLI SORRENTINI AND SORRENTO

Red, white and rosé wines, some of which appear as "Capri," or as "Sorriso di Sorrento," which particularly appeals to the more romantic tourists.

FALERNO

Both dry and sweet, white and red wines come from the plain north of Naples. The white is straw-yellow with a hint of amber and full flavor.

ISCHIA

Ischia Bianco is a delicate white, drunk young and chilled. It is made from a mixture of Biancolella and Fontana grapes. The reds from the island are not quite so individual, some being rather coarse.

LACRIMA CHRISTI

This is a very popular wine because of its memorable name (tears of Christ), but only the dry, German-style white lives up to its reputation. Other wines, including reds and rosés grown on the slopes of Vesuvius, are sold under this name and can be disappointing.

ABRUZZI-MOLISE

Craggy and mountainous, this region is not a great wine producer. What it does produce is either drunk locally or sent north for blending.

ABRUZZI BIANCO

A sharp, fresh white from the Trebbiano grape that makes a good accompaniment to fish.

ABRUZZI ROSSO

From the Montepulciano grape, which is grown widely throughout the region, this is a very light red, sometimes with a slight tingle.

APULIA, BASILICATA, CALABRIA

In the hot south of Italy, wine production is the main source of income — in fact Apulia produces more wine than any other region of Italy. But because of the heavy soil and the fierce sun, and the fact that the vines are grown close to the ground so that extra heat is reflected up at them, the wine tends to be coarse and strong. The reds are used for blending and the whites as a base for the vermouth industry in Turin.

ALEATICO

A rich, sweet dessert wine from the grape of the same name. The must is taken off the skins of part-dried grapes and fermentation is halted by the addition of spirits. The result is quite strong (14°-17°).

CASTEL DEL MONTE

A fresh tingling white wine from the Bombino Bianco grape.

CASTELLANA

Red and rosé wines drunk very young and mainly used for blending.

LOCOROTONDO

Pips and skin are removed from a mixture of grapes to produce a characterless white wine used mainly as a base for vermouth.

*A*malfi was the first
Italian maritime republic
and dates back to the 6th
century (above). It is
famed for its fish
restaurants and one of its
specialties is a dish of
spaghetti with octopus,
anchovies, shrimp and
garlic. These
extraordinary conicle
huts (right), or "trulli", are
a form of dwelling dating
from prehistoric times.
Made of shale rock, trulli
are found only in the area
of Apulia; the town shown
is Alberobello. The flat
sections of roof are used
for drying walnuts in the
sun as well as for hanging
out the washing.

In the rest of the south, the land is mountainous, parched and poor. Olive oil rather than butter is the cooking medium — it costs less to keep an olive tree than a cow, and olive trees survive in poorer soil. Under the searing sun tempers run high, and the food is as fiery as those who eat it. Dried tubular pasta is served with angry sauces of garlic, hot peppers and burning chilies that take a little getting used to before their flavors can be truly appreciated.

The cooking of these poorer regions is largely based on pasta and vegetables, often cooked up together in a substantial soup. Fish soups of all kinds are made round the coast, but transport is difficult through the rocky terrain and fish is not often available inland. Instead, the locals keep chickens which scratch about in the streets, and make imaginative use of their hens' eggs, even combining them with sheep's tripe in one dish.

Sicily and Sardinia

Sicily and Sardinia owe a lot of the distinctiveness of their cooking to the invaders from Greece, Phoenicia and Spain who have occupied the islands over the centuries. Both subsist mainly on a diet of pasta and bread, but Sicily produces early vegetables, olives and citrus fruit as well as wheat, while Sardinia is a pastoral island almost entirely devoted to rearing sheep and, to a lesser extent, goats.

From the Saracens, Sicily learned the art of making delicious sweets and pastries, among them cannoli, filled with cream cheese, chocolate and candied fruit, and cassata, a layered cake which includes the same ingredients plus liqueur, and is sometimes covered in chocolate. Baking is a national pastime in Sicily. There are large loaves like cartwheels and savory buns stuffed with pork, bacon and cheese.

Sardinians bake thin brittle circles of bread called *carta di musica,* music paper, and for weddings there are elaborately iced cakes inscribed with the names of the bride and groom. Sardinians are fond of roasting whole sheep and goats, as well as wild boar, suckling pig and smaller game, on an outdoor spit. Instead of using herbs, they build their fires of aromatic woods, such as juniper or olive, to give the barbecued meat its distinctive flavor.

The island of Sardinia gave its name to the sardine, which swims in its waters along with lobsters and eels — and all these foods are cooked as simply as they were thousands of years ago, by the Ancient Romans and before.

THE WINES OF SICILY AND SARDINIA

Sardinia's inhabitants are unlike mainland Italians, being more somber and reserved Their wines are just as individual, many of them being as strong as sherry without being fortified. The whites are pinkish and the reds so dark as to be called *vini neri* - black wines.

Most of the wines of Sicily are strong and rough as in southernmost Italy, and most are produced in large co-operatives and used for blending. The one major exception is marsala, the distinctive dessert wine very popular throughout Italy as well as abroad.

The production of marsala was set up around 1760 by a Liverpudlian, John Woodhouse, who visited the island and realized that the wine produced there resembled the base wines of port, sherry and madeira.

The dry local white wine is fortified with wine brandy and sweetened with a local sweet wine made with part-dried grapes and unfermented grape juice, heated until it becomes syrupy.

Marsala is drunk as a dessert wine or an aperitif. It is also blended with egg yolks to make the rich, creamy dessert called Zabaglione.

The Italian kitchen is homely and practical rather than sophisticated. Most of the equipment the Italian cook needs is basic and efficient, and essential to any working kitchen. Some of the ingredients too are those to be found in any well-stocked store cupboard, but the majority are redolent of the flavors and tastes unique to Italian cuisine.

THE ITALIAN KITCHEN

The first priority is a good set of sharp knives. There is nothing more frustrating or time-consuming than sawing away at a tough piece of meat or a squashy tomato with a blunt blade. A mezzaluna, a two-handled crescent-shaped knife with a wide blade, is excellent for chopping herbs, onions and garlic.

Choose a chopping board that does not have a join down the middle — the crack will only harbor food — and remember never to leave a wooden board to soak in water or it will warp.

You will need a large saucepan, preferably heavy-bottomed, for cooking pasta. It should hold 5½ quarts water for 1 pound pasta, so the pasta has room to boil without sticking together. Stir it occasionally with a wooden spoon. A slotted spoon is useful for lifting out gnocchi as they cook and rise to the surface, and a colander is essential for draining.

Large ovenproof casseroles and small heavy-bottomed sauce pans for making sauces will probably already be in your kitchen, as will the indispensable cheese grater.

For making pasta, you do not need a pasta machine. Indeed, they can be extremely expensive and quite tricky both to operate and especially to clean. All you need is a large pastry board or a work surface that you can clean easily, a rolling pin, a pastry wheel and cutters, and a sharp knife.

Knives are of the utmost importance to the smooth functioning of an Italian kitchen. **1** *large, sharp chef's knife;* **2** *vegetable paring knife;* **3** *decorative cutter with a corrugated edge;* **4** *fruit knife,* **5** *mezzaluna — a twin-handled, double-bladed chopper;* **6** *cleaver;* **7** *grapefruit knife.*

Many modern Italian kitchens now boast a hand-turned pasta rolling and cutting machine (left). It ensures fine, even threads of tagliatelli and thin, smooth sheets of lasagne. A hand-held rotary cutter and a ravioli tray (above) are very useful for making meat, cheese, or vegetable-filled pastas.

A TREASURY OF INGREDIENTS

Get out of a train anywhere in Italy and a delicious smell will assail your nostrils and proclaim the identity of the city you have arrived in. In Venice, it's fish; in Naples, garlic; and in Bologna, butter. The store cupboard found in the average Italian kitchen similarly bursts with good things, most of them simple, very individual and highly aromatic.

ANCHOVIES

Anchovies are used in cooking all over Italy. You can buy anchovy fillets canned in oil, anchovy paste and anchovy essence, but these are no real substitute for anchovies prepared at home. Whole salt-cured anchovies are sometimes available from Cypriot or Greek delicatessens, as well as specialist Italian shops. They are sold loose in a drum and should be filleted and steeped in oil as soon as possible.

Rinse the anchovies well in cold running water. Cover the work surface or a board with waxed paper, lay the fish on it and scrape off the skin. Remove the dorsal fin and the bones joined to it. Separate the fish into two halves with a knife and remove the spine. Lay the fillets in a shallow dish and cover each layer with olive oil. Make sure the top layer is completely submerged in oil. Store for up to two weeks in the fridge.

Almonds were first brought to Italy by the Arabs and have been an essential ingredient in Italian cakes and pastries ever since.

To peel almonds, plunge them into boiling water. Remove the pan from the heat and leave the almonds in the water until the skins peel off easily. Alternatively, put the almonds in cold water; bring to a boil, drain and peel.

To toast peeled almonds, put them on a baking sheet in a 350°F (170°C) oven. Turn frequently until they are golden brown.

Salted almonds may be served with drinks. Toast the almonds, dip them in lightly beaten egg white and sprinkle with salt and cayenne, if desired. Return to a low oven to dry.

For sugared almonds, a favorite Italian sweet, shell but do not peel the almonds. Caramelize the same weight of sugar as you have almonds. Coat the almonds in the sugar and allow to set. Repeat the operation twice more, so that you have used three times as much sugar as almonds. Finally, dissolve a little gum arabic in water and dip the almonds in it. Spread them out on a wire mesh and leave to dry.

To grind almonds for use in cakes, puddings and pastries, peel the almonds and dry them in the oven without allowing them to brown. Pound them in a mortar with superfine sugar and sieve the resulting powder.

ALMONDS

ANCHOVY BUTTER

Anchovy butter is a delicious spread for use in antipasti. Simply cream together 100g/4 oz butter and 50g/2 oz anchovy paste.

BACCALA

Baccalà is cod preserved in salt. It is sold in drums and should be soaked for at least 24 hours in several changes of cold water before cooking.

ARTICHOKES

The artichoke is an edible thistle and has had a place of honor in kitchen gardens since the Renaissance. The Italians have a huge variety of artichoke recipes, including some for young artichokes eaten whole. Soak artichokes upside down in a bowl of cold water acidulated with vinegar or lemon juice. Cut off the stem near the base of the vegetable and cut the tips cleanly off the leaves. Rub any cut edges with lemon juice.

Bring a large pan of salted, acidulated water to a boil. Put the artichokes in, stem down, bring back to a boil and test after 30 minutes to see if they are done. Tug at a leaf at the base of the largest artichoke — if it comes away easily, the artichokes are done. Drain them upside down in a colander.

To eat, pull away the leaves, beginning at the base. Dip the succulent base of the leaf in the sauce provided and nibble beginning at the base. Dip the succulent base of the leaf in the sauce provided and nibble away the fleshy part. When all the leaves have been removed, discard the choke. Eat the delicious heart of the artichoke with a knife and fork and more of the sauce. To prepare artichokes for stuffing, slice off the top as well as the stem before you boil it.

When it is cooked, remove the inner leaves and the choke so that you are left with a cup.

If only the heart is needed, cook the artichokes in the usual way. Dismantle each artichoke, as if you were eating it, to uncover the heart.

BORLOTTI BEANS

Kidney-shaped beans eaten fresh and dried. They are very pretty, both pods and beans being speckled yellow, through pink to tawny brown. Tender, moist and sweet when cooked, they have a delicate and delicious flavor.

CAPERS

Capers are the small, green, unripe fruit of a climbing plant and have a very individual flavor. They are sold pickled in vinegar. If the vinegar is too strong, you may have to rinse the capers in water before use. Capers are much used in sauces for pasta, meat and fish.

Italy is famous for its coffees — black espresso and pale brown cappuccino, named after the color of the monks' robes. Caffè alla Borgia is a popular mid-morning pick-me-up laced with apricot brandy and sprinkled with cinnamon. You can make Italian coffee at home in a napoletana - a coffee pot that has a water jug inverted on top of it. Fill the water jug, spoon the ground coffee into the filter basket on top of it and fit the coffee pot, inverted, over that. Put the whole contraption on to heat and when the water boils, turn it upside down so that the water filters through the coffee into the pot beneath.

COFFEE

CHEESES

A salad of mozzarella and tomato, sprinkled with basil.

Parmesan is the best-known of all Italian cheeses. It accompanies pasta and rice and is ideal for cooking because it does not turn stringy as it melts. It is also delicious at the end of a meal with fruit. If you can avoid it, never buy pre-grated parmesan sold in cartons — it has no taste. Parmesan bought by the chunk should be pale yellow and finely honeycombed — the generic name for this cheese in Italy is grana, referring to its fine grain. The best grana is four years old and correspondingly expensive. Store large pieces of parmesan wrapped in two or three sheets of foil in the bottom of the fridge.

Bel paese is a creamy cheese from Lombardy, but with a very mild flavor. It can be used in cooking instead of mozzarella.

Fontina comes from Piedmont. It is a very fat, creamy cheese full of small holes and traditionally used to make fonduta, a non-alcoholic fondue.

Gorgonzola is a veined cow's milk cheese from Lombardy. It has a strong flavor and a beautifully creamy texture. The greenish streaks are developed during maturation in caves or in ageing rooms where the temperature and humidity of the caves is reproduced. Gorgonzola is often eaten creamed with butter and spread on bread.

Mascarpone is a small, double-cream cheese sold in a cheesecloth parcel and eaten with sugar and fruit.

Genuine mozzarella cheeses come from Campania and Apulia and are made with buffalo milk. True mozzarrella is increasingly difficult to get hold of because of the scarcity of the buffalo. The cheese commonly available today is made from cow's milk. It should be eaten absolutely fresh and moist and is sold in round balls wrapped in waxed paper to keep it that way. If the cheese has dried out a little, it is best used in cooking or to top pizzas.

Pecorino is a sheep's milk cheese that can be used for cooking when mature. It has a piquant taste that increases with age and is produced in many regions of Italy including Tuscany, where it is delicate and creamy, and Sicily, where it can be smoked, salted, or flavored with ground pepper or saffron.

Provola and provolone are also buffalo cheeses from Campania and come in different sizes and shapes. Tangier than mozzarella, they can be used in the same way. Cacio a cavallo (or caciocavallo) is a similar cheese and gets its name from the way the cheeses are strung up in pairs "astride" a rod to mature.

Ricotta is a moist curd cheese made from sheep's milk and can be either mild or strong, according to region. In Piedmont and around Rome it is eaten very fresh with pepper and salt, or sometimes with coffee and sugar sprinkled on it. It can be used in cooking sweet and savory dishes. In southern Italy ricotta forte is made from salted sheep's milk. It can be dried in the sun or in an oven and grated for cooking.

A selection of typical Italian cheeses; **1** *parmesan (grana);* **2** *pecorino;* **3** *fontina;* **4** *gorgonzola.*

FROGS

Frog meat is very popular in Italy, especially in the north where an abundance of frogs is found in the rice fields. Frogs have tender, delicate white flesh, which is easily digested and considered to be very good for invalids. It can be fried, with or without batter, or made into a delicious risotto.

GARNISHES FOR SOUPS

Soup is often a substantial dish in Italy and the garnishes are correspondingly hearty. Choose from pasta shapes, bread croûtons — fried or baked in the oven, and sometimes stuffed as well — or dumplings made of potato or semolina and mixed with spinach, chicken, ham or fish and béchamel sauce.

FUNGHI

In the fall, Italians go mushroom hunting for porcini (cepes) which are very fleshy and can be served instead of a meat course. Strict laws govern the quantity and size of mushrooms a person may pick, and anyone finding a fungus of dubious species may have it checked by the authorities. Many different varieties of mushroom grow wild — the market at Trento sells 230 species. Mushrooms not eaten fresh can be dried for use during the rest of the year. Dried mushrooms should be soaked in warm water for a few minutes and not be cooked too long in a dish or they will lose their flavor.

CHICKPEAS

Chickpeas are often served in Italy with pasta (in a dish called tuoni e lampo — thunder and lightning) or in soups. The dried ones should be soaked for 48 hours and simmered for between two and six hours until tender. As this is a lengthy process, it may be wiser to buy the canned variety.

Ice cream originated in the Near East but today the world specialists in making ice cream are the Italians — especially the Neapolitans. The Italians were always partial to a cooling end to a meal — in Ancient Rome snow was brought down from the mountains and flavored with crushed fruit.

In modern times the Italians became famous for their ice creams first in Paris, where the Neapolitan, Tortoni, created biscuit tortoni as well as a variety of gelati and granite in his ice cream parlor on the Boulevard des Italiens.

GELATI

GNOCCHI

These are dumplings made from semolina or potato. The singular, gnoccho, means numbskull or puddinghead, and gnocchi are a bit plain and stodgy on their own. They are usually eaten in a soup or with a sauce as an accompaniment to a meat dish. A very cheap and tasty meal is gnocchi baked in the oven with layers of cheese and tomato sauce. For recipes, see pp. 57-59.

HAZELNUTS

To peel hazelnuts, shell them and toast in a 350°F(180°C) oven until golden beneath skins. Wrap them in a terry — cloth dishtowel and rub briskly to remove the skin.

KID

Kid and suckling lamb (abbacchio) are great delicacies in Italy. They are also very expensive because they are slaughtered so young. At 9 pounds they have tender white meat; at 22 pounds it is a delicate pink. They should be eaten shortly after slaughter.

The prince of herbs, basil.

HERBS

Wild herbs grow in profusion on Italian hillsides and have been used in Italian cooking at least since the days of Ancient Rome. Most popular are marjoram, sage, rosemary, thyme, parsley, bay and, of course, basil. Basil has a special affinity with tomatoes and, pounded with garlic, olive oil, parmesan and pine nuts, makes the wonderful Genoese speciality pesto, the most aromatic pasta sauce of all.

MARINADES

A quick and delicious marinade for meat to be broiled can be made of oil and lemon juice, or from white wine mixed with chopped herbs and seasoned with salt and pepper. Add a dash of brandy, if you like it, and marinate steaks, chops and cubes for an hour or two.

Marinate larger cuts of meat for several days (according to age and toughness) in a non-metallic bowl in the fridge. Turn the meat occasionally using a wooden spoon. For the marinade you will need a mixture of· white wine and wine vinegar and a selection of chopped vegetables and parsley stems.

Alternatively, you can use a cooked marinade. Fry chopped vegetables gently in oil, add wine and vinegar, using a little more vinegar than you would in an uncooked marinade, and bring to a boil. Simmer for 30 minutes, allow to cool, then pour over the meat.

POLENTA

Polenta has, in one form or another, been a staple Italian food for thousands of years. Today it is mainly made of yellow cornmeal and often takes the place of bread in Lombardy and Veneto. The meal is boiled in water until it is thick, then poured onto a board and left to cool; then it is cut into slices that are eaten cold, fried, or served with sauce. Recipes on p. 59.

OLIVE OIL

Olive oil is one of the oldest and most popular culinary oils. The quality of the oil depends not on the quality of the olive but on its processing; the more refined the oil the lighter its color and flavor. **1** pure olive oil which, although refined, retains some of its olive flavor and is widely used as a salad oil; **2** fine olive oil, refined further than pure olive oil, this type is not suitable for salads but is ideal for frying; **3** extra virgin olive oil is the best for salads. Taken from the first cold pressing of the olive, it is full of the flavor promised by its rich color.

O live oil is the major cooking medium around the Ligurian coast, in Tuscany and southern Italy. The best oil is said to come from Lucca in Tuscany. The first pressing of the olives produces a rich, fruity, green oil that is preferred by the cognoscenti to the mellower, more golden variety produced later on. Sadly, oil for export is often blended for uniformity and much of its character is lost.

Buy the most expensive olive oil you can afford for use on salads and in cooking dishes where its strong flavor is a component part of the dish. Where the flavor would be obtrusive, substitute a cheaper tasteless oil such as peanut oil. The best olive oil is too good and too expensive to be used indiscriminately.

PISTACHIO

P eel pistachio nuts by dropping them into boiling salted water for a few seconds; the salt helps the nuts keep their green color. Remove the pan from the heat and let the nuts soak for a minute before peeling off the skins.

PINE NUTS

T hese come from the cones of the stone pine and are usually available from health food stores and delicatessens. They are small and creamy colored with a sweet, delicate flavor. They are used in pesto and sweet and sour (agrodolce) sauces as well as in sweet cakes and cookies.

PASTA

Taste in pasta divides Italy roughly into two. In the north of Italy and as far south as Rome the pasta is mainly of the ribbon variety — flat, fresh and home-made with egg. Around Naples and further south it is tubular, eggless, mass produced and dried.

Pasta for soups includes conchigliette (little shells), anellini (little hoops), nocchette (little bows) and semini (little seeds).

Pasta to be boiled includes fettucine (ribbons), fusilli (spirals), spaghetti, ziti (fat spaghetti), conchiglie (shells), penne (nibs), cappelletti (hats), farfalle (bows), macaroni and ruote (wheels).

Pasta to be stuffed includes lumache (snails), cannelloni, ravioli, and tortellini.

Instructions for making fresh pasta can be found on pp. 51-56.

First column, top to bottom:
1 whole wheat bucatini, **2** creste; **3** lumaconi; **4** green bigoli; **5** lasagne.

Second column, top to bottom:
6 maccheroncini (frilled macaroni); **7** sedanini; **8** vegetable macaroni; **9** long fusilli; **10** tagliatelli, fettucine.

Third column, top to bottom:
11 *semolina spaghetti;* **12** *lumachine;* **13** *marille;* **14** *viti;* **15** *zite.*

Fourth column, top to bottom:
16 *large macaroni;* **17** *elbow macaroni;* **18** *penne;* **19** *green viti;* **20** *reginelle;* **21** *pappardelle.*

Fifth column, top to bottom:
22 *whole wheat spaghetti;* **23** *farfalle;* **24** *canelloni;* **25** *trenitte;* **26** *thin pappardelle or mafaldine.*

QUAIL

Quail are becoming increasingly available in American markets. They usually weigh from 3 to 6 ounces; you'll probably want to allow two per person.

Sardines are known by many different names in Italy. The Italians say the sardine has 24 virtues and loses one every hour — therefore it should be eaten very fresh. To prepare fresh sardines, slit open the stomach and pull out entrails and the backbone. Cut off the head, if preferred. Fresh sardines are delicious broiled over an open fire with a little rosemary, black pepper and lemon juice or dipped in flour, egg and breadcrumbs and fried.

RICE

Italy is Europe's biggest rice producer. Piedmont and Lombardy are the regions where it is grown. Italian rice has shorter, fatter grains than the Asian variety. It takes a little longer to cook, but has more bite and body and is excellent for risotto and for soups where the grains must remain firm and creamy as well as succulent. Arborio is the variety usually exported. Asian rice is better for timbales, salads and pilafs, because it can be cooked until it is dry and fluffy.

SAFFRON

Saffron gives its lovely color to Milan's famous risotto. It comes from the pistils of the autumn-flowering crocus. Half a million pistils are needed to make about 2 pounds of saffron powder, so it is very expensive.

SARDINES

This sharp green sauce is often served with boiled meats and with white fish. Use vinegar for a meat sauce and lemon juice for a fish one. Blend together $\frac{1}{4}$ cup olive oil and 1 tablespoon each of parsley and capers, 2 anchovy fillets, $\frac{1}{2}$ clove garlic and 1 teaspoon either red wine vinegar or lemon juice.

RADICCHIO

A specialty of Treviso, radicchio is shaped like a small round lettuce, but is rose-colored with cream veins. Radicchio from Castelfranco has darker streaks against a lighter ground. Purists say the two should never be mixed.

SALSA VERDE

SAUSAGES AND COOKED MEATS

*E*ach region of Italy has its special kind of salami. Sometimes the meat is fine ground, giving a smooth texture and a pale pink color, or it may be coarse ground so that the sausage has large chunks of dark red and white meat, often dotted with black peppercorns.

Luganega is made from pork shoulder, parmesan and a little spice. A mild sausage with a high meat content, it is sold in continuous coils.

Mortadella is Italy's most famous sausage. It is made of different cuts of pork and comes from Bologna. Delicate in both taste and texture, it varies in size, sometimes reaching the astonishing girth of 18 inches.

Pancetta is the same cut of pork as bacon, but cured in salt and spices instead of being smoked. It is rolled into a sausage shape and sold sliced.

Parma ham, prosciutto, is made from the boned hind legs of the pig. It is first salted and then dried — the air in the hills around Parma being ideal to bring it to maturity. It is sliced paper thin. The tender, sweet, light red meat is popularly served as an appetizer with fresh figs or melon.

Zampone is a specialty of Modena — the boned foreleg of the pig stuffed with ground spiced pork. It is boiled and served sliced with other boiled meats.

Italian smoked and cured meats are delicious as antipasti or as cocktail snacks, and make exceptionally toothsome sandwiches. Above, top to bottom: prosciutto crudo — a delicate raw ham; "Hungarian" salami; salt beef; pastrami — cured and smoked beef; a pale, marbled liver sausage; Milan salami; and mortadella — the fine-textured sausage of Bologna, often speckled with pistachio nuts.

SHERBET

The Arabs brought the art of sherbet making to Italy. Sherbets are light ices made with fruit juice, wine or liqueurs (never cream or eggs) and are served as soon as they are frozen in tall glasses, perhaps with a trickle of wine or liqueur poured over. They used to be eaten between courses to refresh the palate, but are more common today as a dessert.

SEMOLINA

This is a flour — from coarse-ground durum wheat — used to make gnocchi. Durum wheat is also used in the manufacture of commercial pasta. Don't confuse it with the grain of the same name used to make a milk pudding.

TUNA

Canned tuna, in oil or water, is a useful item to have on hand for the delicious Tuscan salad of tonno e fagioli tuna and white beans. Simply mix the two together with a little chopped onion and perhaps some parsley, and season with pepper.

SQUID

Squid comes from the cephalopod family, along with octopus. To prepare it, pull the head gently away from the body. Discard the "pen" and remove the pinkish purple skin from the body. Wash the body and cut it into rings. The fins are also edible. Cut off the tentacles and cut them into short lengths. Discard the head and the entrails.

Though an indispensable ingredient in Italian cooking, the tomato was introduced into the country only comparatively recently. The Italians grow either plum tomatoes or the huge, curved, irregular Marmande variety — both have infinitely more flavor than the pale, insipid specimens cultivated in America. Many Italians bottle their own tomatoes and make their own tomato concentrate at home for use during the winter months. Those who have neither the time nor the space use the canned variety. (There are recipes for home-made tomato sauce on pp. 45-47).

Spices have been used in Italian cooking since Roman times and during the Renaissance Venice was at the center of the spice trade between the Far East and Europe.

Nutmeg is used in savory and sweet dishes that contain spinach or ricotta. Cloves are found in the rich panforte of Siena, vanilla sugar in sweet pastries and creams.

SPICES

This is wind-dried cod and should not be confused with baccalà, salt cod. Stockfish (from the Norwegian stock, for stick, as it is dried wound around poles) is sold hanging up in the shop. Beat the stockfish with a pestle to break down the fibers and soak it until tender enough to cook. As preparation is so lengthy, it is not surprising that this fish has never become popular in America.

STOCKFISH

TRUFFLES

Truffles grow in Tuscany, Romagna and Piedmont and are hunted by dogs specially trained to sniff them out during the truffle season, which runs from October to March. They are eaten raw, sliced on risotto or fonduta, or cooked in butter and served under a mound of freshly grated parmesan.

VARIETY MEAT

All kinds of variety meats are popular in Italy, including calf's head, pigs' feet, tripe, tongue and lung. Calf's brains and sweetbreads (the thymus gland) are especially prized delicacies. Brains should be washed thoroughly under cold running water, then soaked in cold water for ten minutes. Drain; remove the blood vessels and membranes. Simmer for about 20 minutes in salted acidulated water to which you have added some carrot, onion and celery, then drain and allow to cool. Refrigerate until firm. Slice the brains thickly, dip in egg and then in breadcrumbs and fry briefly in oil over high heat until golden. Drain on paper towels and serve with lemon wedges.

Italians do not feel it necessary to soak sweetbreads for hours in several changes of water until all the blood has disappeared. They should be washed under cold running water, when most of the membrane can be removed. They can then be cooked as for brains, above.

TOMATO

VEAL

Vitello is meat from a milk-fed calf slaughtered at three weeks. Vitellone is meat from an older, grass-fed, non-working animal. Beef comes from a working animal, the ox (manzo) and not from the cow (mucca). To make perfect scaloppine you need good veal cut into thin slices across the grain. Then the scaloppine should be pounded to make them thinner and flatter. The idea is not to hammer at them indiscriminately, but to bring the mallet down and slide it forward at the same time, stretching the meat. Turn the meat as you go and stretch it evenly all around.

BASIC RECIPES

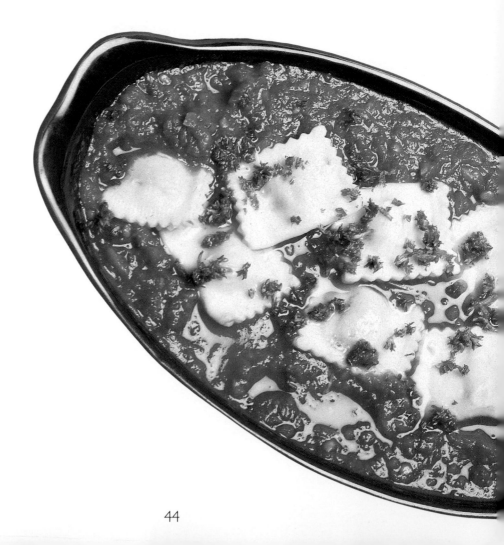

SALSA DI POMODORO
Basic tomato sauce

Ingredients/makes 4 large jars	I small head garlic
	8 whole cloves
14 lbs ripe tomatoes	Salt
2 lbs medium onions	Olive oil
2 lbs slender carrots	
1 ¾ cups sliced celery	
¾ cup mixed chopped parsley, sage and basil	

U se this sauce to flavor soups and as a base for other sauces, or just heat it up and use on its own. Wash the tomatoes well and seed them, then chop coarsely. Put in a large pan, preferably stainless steel. Coarsely chop onions and carrot; add to pan with celery and herbs. Peel head of garlic; add garlic and whole cloves to pan. Heat gently, and as soon as it starts to simmer, reduce heat, cover and cook for 2½ hours, stirring occasionally. If tomatoes are very watery, drain after 30 minutes and continue to cook. Do not let any condensed water from the lid drop into sauce when you lift lid. Make sure sauce does not stick to pan. When sauce is cooked, press it through a strainer into a large pan and lightly salt it. Add 1 cup olive oil and cook for 1 hour longer. Pour sauce into canning jars, seal and process in a pressure cooker according to manufacturer's instructions.

*R*avioli makes a mouthwatering first course, whether served steaming hot in a cooked tomato sauce or chilled in a thick salsa of strained and herbed fresh tomato pulp.

SALSA DI POMODORO PICCANTE
Piquant tomato sauce

Ingredients/serves 4	
2¾ lbs firm, ripe tomatoes	1 bay leaf
4 medium green bell peppers	Salt
1 small red bell pepper	1 cup white wine vinegar
1 pickled pepper	2 tablespoons sugar
¾ cup sliced onions	Olive oil
2 whole cloves	
1 cinnamon stick	

T his sauce is similar to tomato ketchup and makes a good accompaniment to roast and boiled meats and hard-cooked eggs. Halve and seed tomatoes, place in a large pan (not an aluminium pan). Halve and seed bell peppers, add to tomatoes. Add pickled pepper, onions, cloves, cinnamon stick, bay leaf and 1 teaspoon salt. Stir well and simmer for 3 hours over very low heat. Make sure condensation on pan lid does not drip into sauce. Use a cloth or paper towels to soak it up when you lift lid. After 3 hours, remove pan from heat, rub mixture through a strainer, discarding cloves, bay leaf and cinnamon stick. Return to pan, add vinegar and sugar and simmer over very low heat for about 2 hours. Cool sauce, then pour into 5 small jars; cover sauce in each jar with about ¼ inch oil. Add lids and store sauce in refrigerator. Or pour hot sauce into canning jars, seal and process in a pressure cooker according to maufacturer's instructions.

SALSA DI POMODORO CON CARNE

Tomato and meat sauce

Makes 9 lbs sauce	¼ cup butter
8 lbs firm, ripe tomatoes	⅓ cup olive oil
1 lb slender carrots	1 ¾ lbs lean ground beef
¾ cup sliced celery	Salt
½ cup mixed chopped parsley, sage and basil	
5 cloves garlic, crushed	
1 lb onions, thinly sliced	

C ook tomato sauce as directed on page 45, using tomatoes, carrots, celery, herbs and garlic. Put the onions in a pan with butter and olive oil. Heat gently until softened, add meat and cook for 1 ½ hours, adding a little tomato juice if necessary. Combine meat sauce with tomato sauce and cook for 1 hour longer, then season with salt. Pour hot sauce into canning jars, seal and process in a pressure cooker according to manufacturer's directions.

Each serving of spaghetti should be topped with just enough sauce to flavor and moisten it, but the texture of the pasta should predominate.

BAGNA CAUDA
Hot anchovy dip

Ingredients/serves 4	2 tablespoons butter
½ cup flat anchovy fillets	¾ cup virgin olive oil
5 cloves garlic	Salt

Bagna cauda is a hot dip, a specialty of Piedmont. It is brought to the table in a terra cotta saucepan and put over a little candle — if possible each person should have his or her own chafing dish. Each person dips crudités or cooked vegetables into the sauce. Use tender white cardoons — a relative of the thistle and the artichoke — soaked first in acidulated cold water; peppers, celery, tender cauliflower etc, or cooked onions, potatoes, beets, carrots and turnips, etc. Make sure the bagna cauda dish is stable to avoid accidents. If you want the garlic to be more digestible, soak it for 2 hours before use in a glass of milk. In some parts of Piedmont it is customary to add crushed pieces of walnut to the dip. Leftovers of the sauce can be served with scrambled eggs. Rinse anchovies well, then pat dry. Cut the garlic into fine slivers or, if preferred, crush it. Put pan over a low flame and add the butter and garlic. Let it cook gently for a few minutes without browning, then gradually add oil and the anchovies. Blend anchovies in well and cook over a very low flame for about 15 minutes, stirring occasionally. Finally taste and add salt, if necessary. Serve in the cooking dish.

PESTO ALLA GENOVESE
Basil and garlic sauce

Ingredients/serves 4	1 teaspoon pinenuts *or* a well-peeled walnut half
About 30 fresh basil leaves	
Salt	1 tablespoon grated parmesan cheese
3 cloves garlic, peeled	
	Virgin olive oil

The Ligurians say that the basil should be grown in Liguria! If possible, use the top leaves of the basil plant. Gently wash the basil leaves and pat as dry as possible; put them in a mortar (a marble one is preferable), add a pinch of salt (to help the basil retain its vivid green colour), the garlic, pine nuts or walnut.

Crush all the ingredients with a pestle, gradually adding parmesan (this will prevent the paste slipping out of the mortar) and pecorino. If you prefer, use extra parmesan instead of the pecorino and another tablespoon of olive oil. When you have a smooth paste, add 2-3 tablespoons olive oil, mixing well with a wooden spoon. The pesto is then ready to serve. When using pesto to flavor pasta, dilute it first with a spoonful of pasta cooking water or a chunk of cold butter to thin it a little. If it is to be used to flavor minestrone, dilute it with a spoonful of soup and then add to the minestrone just before taking it from the heat.

*F*resh basil provides a brilliant green color and an inimitable flavor. If it is not available, parsley will provide a green sauce with quite a different emphasis.

PASTA

A 1 pound package of dried pasta will serve five people. Bring 5½ quarts water to a boil in a large saucepan. Add a pinch of salt and about 1 teaspoon oil. Add pasta and increase heat to get the water back to boiling point as quickly as possible. Cook it at a full rolling boil, stirring occasionally with a wooden spoon, for about 10 minutes. Remember that pasta continues to cook for a few moments when you take it off the heat so allow for this by stopping when pasta is just al dente. When it is ready, add a cup or two of cold water to stop cooking and then drain. Meticulous draining is not necessary, as pasta should not dry out. (Italians say pasta is greedy for water.) The process is exactly the same for fresh pasta, but you will need about ½ pound pasta per person, and the cooking time will be only about 4 minutes.

Using a pasta machine

The dough should be firmer than for hand-rolled pasta. Feed dough into the machine in small pieces, each rolled in flour, so it will not be so likely to stick to the blades.

PASTA FATTA IN CASA
Homemade pasta

Ingredients/serves 4	4 medium eggs
3½ cups all-purpose flour	Vegetable oil

Dust board or working surface with flour. Mound flour (which should be as fresh as possible) onto the board and make a well in center. Break eggs into it. (Any shell will ruin pasta.) Add 1 tablespoon cold water to eggs and 1 or 2 teaspoons oil. Beat eggs with a fork and gradually work in flour, using your hands when dough becomes stiff. Knead for at least 10 minutes. Dough should be stiff — add extra flour if it is too soft. When little air bubbles start to appear, roll dough into a ball, flatten then roll out with a rolling pin as far as possible, making sure that thickness is uniform.

Step-by-step below

1 Make a well in the mound of flour, break in the eggs and beat with a fork.

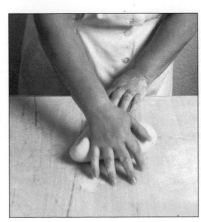

2 Gradually work in flour. When the dough stiffens, carry on using your hands.

3 Knead vigorously for at least 10 minutes.

4 When bubbles appear, roll the dough into a ball and then flatten it.

Continued over page

Roll out with a rolling pin. Starting from the centre, roll out in all directions.

5

6 Turn dough around, using a rolling pin.

Put it back down on the board and continue to roll out in the other direction.

7

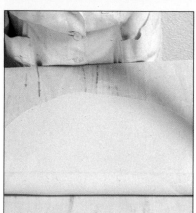

PASTA ROSSA
Red pasta

Ingredients/serves 4	1 ¾ cups all-purpose flour
½ lb carrots	3 eggs
1 teaspoon tomato paste	Pinch of salt

T he amount of flour used here will vary according to the moisture content of the carrots. Peel and steam carrots and press through a fine strainer into a pan. Put pan over heat and stir with a wooden spoon to dry out the pureé. Stir in tomato paste and let it cool. Proceed as with egg pasta (p.51), adding carrot mixture to eggs in flour well. Add more flour if necessary. This pasta, like the spinach variety, does not roll out as thinly as basic pasta dough. Treat it like plain egg pasta. Using three colors of pasta, you can prepare harlequin pasta.

PASTA VERDE
Green pasta

Ingredients/serves 4	1 ¾ cups all-purpose flour
½ cup very well-drained cooked spinach	3 eggs

ress spinach through a strainer or purée in a blender. Make dough as usual, add spinach and knead for 10 minutes. If dough is too soft, add a little more flour. It is difficult to stretch out green pasta very thinly.

TAGLIATELLE

Tagliatelle is the simplest pasta shape to make — therefore it is probably the most commonly found. Make the pasta — white, red or green — as directed in the preceding pages. Roll out as thinly as possible, then beginning at one end, roll the dough into a long, thin cylinder. Beginning at one end, cut the roll into slices, rather like cutting refrigerator cookies. When the roll has been cut into slices, gently ease the slices into separate strands of tagliatelle.

Step-by-step below

1 Using a knife with a wide blade, cut roll into slices of desired thickness.

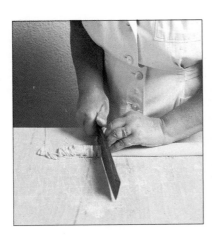

2 Separate and spread out pasta shapes on board.

AGNOLINI

P roceed as for tagliatelle (see p.53), making the dough a little firmer as it is to be rolled out more thinly. Cut squares 1 inch wide for serving in soup, otherwise 2 inches wide. Fill generously with stuffing and fold the pasta over. Put your index finger against the side of pasta envelope and curve pasta, joining the two ends. There should be a little hole in the center of the agnolino. *Step-by-step 1-3 below*

Cut pasta into strips 1 inch wide and place strips on top of one another. **1**

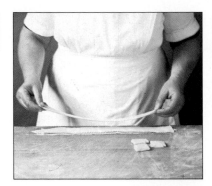

2 Using a sharp knife, cut strips into squares.

Put your index finger against side where the pasta was folded and turn two ends round your finger. **3**

1 To make cappell-etti, use your hands and not the board.

CAPPELLETTI

I t is thought this pasta shape got its name from the alpine hats it resembles. Prepare the pasta as for tagliatelle (see p.53), and let it rest under a cloth. Using a little serrated cutter or a sharp knife, cut pasta into squares with 1-1½-inch-long sides. Place a pea-sized amount of filling in the middle of each square, then fold into a triangle. Then, keeping left index finger under filling, join the two points of the triangle, making sure that there is no hole (unlike agnolini). Stretch sideways a little, if necessary. *Step 1 above*

CAPPELLETTI TOSCANI

Prepare pasta with a little less egg (3 eggs to 3½ cups flour). When dough has been rolled out, cut out circles. Put meat filling in center of each circle. Fold circle in half to make a semicircle. Holding the shape in your hands (not on the board) press edges around filling, then join the two points of the half-moon shape. Do not turn pasta up around filling but leave it as it is, as though it were the brim of a little hat. There should be a small hole in center.

Step-by-step below

1 Cut out circles on rolled out dough, place meat filling on top, and fold in half.

2 Close edges around filling and press seal flat. Join corners of half circles together.

ANOLINI

These are a Bolognese specialty. Roll out dough and cut out 2-inch circles. Fill with a nut-sized piece of meat filling and fold over free pasta, making a little rim on the lower semicircle. Press rim around filling and then, as for agnolini, shape pasta around your left index finger.

RAVIOLI

These are common to all parts of Italy. They can be made with plain or egg pasta and are much like tortellini (see next page). Make them square or round.

Note, instructions on next page <u>do not</u> tell you how to make ravioli in the traditional fashion, by rolling pasta into a sheet, dotting with filling, and topping with a second sheet.

TORTELLINI AND TORTELLONI

P repare pasta as before and roll out. Cover pasta with a cloth to avoid drying out, except in the area where you will be working. There are two basic tortellini shapes: square — like ravioli — and curved triangles with the edges joined. When these are large and served as a first course in sauce instead of in a broth, they are often called tortelloni. Both plain and green tortellini/tortelloni are popular. Below is a simple version of tortelloni verde al gratin.

Step-by-step below

Place a nut-sized piece of filling — either meat or ricotta and spinach — toward one corner of a square of pasta.

1

2 Fold the top over to form a triangle and join the points together to make a curved shape.

Place the tortelloni in a shallow dish and cover with a quantity of homemade tomato sauce.

3

4 Cover with a thick layer of mozzarella cheese. Cook for 45 minutes or until bubbling, then serve.

GNOCCHI DI PATATE
Potato dumplings

First recipe/serves 4	Second recipe/serves 4
1¼ lbs russet potatoes	1 lb russet potatoes
1 teaspoon salt	1 teaspoon salt
1 tablespoon grappa, if desired	2 eggs
1 egg	1¼ cups all-purpose flour
1 cup all-purpose flour	

These gnocchi can be served with butter and parmesan, sage butter or a tomato sauce, meat sauce or pesto. Peel potatoes and boil them in salted water over low heat. Use even-sized potatoes, so that they cook evenly. When just tender, drain, and while still hot mash and put onto a board. Make a well in the middle of mashed potatoes and put in the salt, grappa if using, and egg (or eggs). Then pour on flour and mix well to give a firm dough that does not stick to hands. The amount of flour will vary depending on how moist potatoes are. Knead dough for some minutes. Cut off a piece of dough and roll into a cylinder on floured board. Cut off 1-inch slices, roll into balls and flour well. Take a grater (or fork) and decorate dumplings with holes or ridges, pressing in with your finger on one side to give a shell shape. Bring a large pan of salted water to a boil and gently put in all the gnocchi at once. When they come to surface and float, remove with a slotted spoon, keeping the water boiling, and put in a casserole dish. Pour over hot sauce of your choice, sprinkle with parmesan, add a second layer of gnocchi etc. Put a cover on the dish and place over a saucepan of boiling water to let gnocchi absorb the flavour of the sauce. *Step-by-step below*

Mash potatoes, mix in other ingredients and blend well.

1

2

Cut dough into pieces, rolling out each one by hand.

Continued over page

Continued from previous page

3 Cut each piece into 1-inch slices, flour and mark with fork prongs on one side.

4 They can also be pressed against the reverse side of a grater.

GNOCCHI DI SEMOLINA

1 Pour the cooked semolina into a wide dish or onto a marble slab which has been lightly oiled.

2 With a metal spatula, spread to about ½-inch thickness.

3 With a cookie cutter or glass, cut dough into discs.

4 Lift up gnocchi and lay in a buttered dish.

Both semolina and potato gnocchi are favorites of northern Italy. They are particularly popular as a dish for meatless holy days and Fridays.

GNOCCHI DI SEMOLINA
Semolina dumplings

Ingredients/serves 4	6 tablespoons parmesan cheese
3½ cups milk	2 egg yolks
Salt	Pepper
¾ cup fine semolina	Pinch of ground nutmeg
½ cup butter	Breadcrumbs

These are sometimes thought to be a Roman specialty, but in fact they are eaten all over Italy. Heat milk with a pinch of salt, and when it boils gradually add semolina, stirring the whole time with a wooden spoon to avoid lumps. Continue to cook, stirring, for 20 minutes. Remove from heat and add 2 tablespoons butter in small pieces. Then gradually stir in 2 tablespoons parmesan cheese, the egg yolks, one at a time, a pinch of pepper and nutmeg. Oil 1 or 2 large dishes or a clean marble kitchen slab and pour semolina mixture on. Spread out to ½-inch thickness using a cold wet spatula and allow to cool. Preheat oven to 350°F (175°C). Melt remaining 6 tablespoons butter; use some of butter to grease the casserole you want to cook and serve gnocchi in. Cut out squares or circles of semolina dough and place in greased dish. Drizzle with butter and sprinkle with parmesan, add a second layer of gnocchi, and so on. Sprinkle breadcrumbs over gnocchi and bake for about 20 minutes or until golden brown.

Step-by-step, page 58

POLENTA

Polenta can be made either from finely-ground cornmeal, coarser cornmeal or from buckwheat flour. The best pan for polenta is a copper one with a convex bottom to make stirring easier. Polenta should be cooked in the proportion of 1½ cups cornmeal to 6¼ cups salted water, and this should not come more than halfway up the saucepan. The quantities vary according to how it is to be served. If a sauce is to be served with it, for four people you will need 3½ cups cornmeal and 11¼ cups water. For coarse meal, boil the water, then add meal gradually in handfuls, stirring to avoid lumps. The cooking time will vary from 40 minutes to about an hour. Stir the mixture constantly, scraping sides and bottom. When polenta comes away easily from sides of the pan at end of cooking time, loosen it from pan with a slotted spoon moistened in cold water, and turn

Continued on next page

Continued from previous page

out. Serve the polenta very hot. If you use finer cornmeal, add a fifth of it to the cold water before putting it on to boil, then cover the pan and bring to a boil. Boil for 10 minutes, then gradually add the rest and proceed as before.

PASTA PER PIZZA
Pizza dough

Ingredients/serves 4	1 cup all-purpose flour
1 cake compressed yeast or 1 package active day yeast	Pinch of salt

Pizza is not commonly made at home it Italy, but eaten in a pizzeria. It is a specialty of Naples. Crumble yeast into a cup and dissolve in about ¼ cup lukewarm water (95°F, 35°C). For dry yeast, use warm water (110°F, 45°C). Mix in about ¼ cup flour, cover cup with a cloth and leave in a warm place to rise. Put remaining flour into a bowl, add a pinch of salt and put yeast mixture in a well in the middle. Work in yeast mixture gradually, adding just enough water to make dough smooth and pliable. Knead for 10 minutes, then roll dough into a ball, put in a floured bowl, cover and let rise in a warm place until dough has doubled in bulk. Once risen, the dough is ready to be made into pizzas. For homemade pizza you can buy ready-made bread dough, to which you just need to add 1 tablespoon oil, knead and roll out. This is a much quicker method than making pizza dough from scratch.

Step-by-step below

1 Measure the fresh or dried yeast and the flour carefully. Sieve the flour into a large bowl.

2 Make a well in the center of the flour and pour in the yeast mixture and a little lukewarm water.

Using a palette knife or spatula, mix until you have a firm, plastic dough. If extra water is required, work in carefully to avoid dough becoming sticky. **3**

4 Turn dough out onto a floured board and knead vigorously for 10 minutes.

Place the dough in a lightly floured bowl. Cover with plastic wrap. Put in a warm place and allow to double in bulk **5**

6 Turn the risen dough onto a floured board. Knead and punch down until all air pockets are eliminated. The dough should be smooth, firm and elastic.

Right: Pizza alla Napoletana; for recipe, see p.112.

ANTI PASTI

Antipasti are savoury morsels designed to whet the appetite. Serve an attractive arrangement of eggs, olives, pickled vegetables, artichoke hearts, asparagus, and anchovies, or paper-thin slices of prosciutto with melon or figs, or choose from any of the following recipes.

Mousse di Pomodoro in Gelatina
Jellied tomato mousse

Ingredients/serves 4	I envelope unflavored gelatin
I lb tomatoes, peeled, seeded, chopped	¼ cup dry sherry
	1 ¾ cups beef stock
Salt	About ½ pint whipping cream
¼ cup thick béchamel sauce	(I cup), whipped

LAZIO, UMBRIA AND THE MARCHES

Purée tomatoes in a blender or press through a strainer, season with salt and cook gently for 5 minutes. Put to drain in a cloth tied up at 4 corners over a bowl for 2½ hours. Mix drained tomatoes thoroughly with béchamel sauce; press through a strainer or process in a blender. Refrigerate for 20 minutes. Meanwhile, soften gelatin in sherry. Heat stock in a small pan; add softened gelatin and stir over low heat until completely dissolved. Chill until syrupy and slightly thickened. Pour half the gelatin mixture into a glass bowl and swirl to cover sides. Chill until set (do not refrigerate remaining gelatin mixture). Mix tomato mixture with a wooden spoon to give a soft, smooth consistency. Fold in whipped cream. Spoon into gelatin-coated bowl. If necessary, stir remaining gelatin mixture over low heat until liquefied; then pour over tomato mixture. Chill until set. Unmold onto a serving dish and serve.　　*Photograph page 66*

Pomodori Alla Siciliana
Baked stuffed tomatoes

Ingredients/serves 4	3 tablespoons capers
8 large ripe tomatoes	2 tablespoons breadcrumbs
I onion, finely chopped	¼ cup sliced ripe olives
Vegetable oil	Salt and pepper
8 anchovy fillets, rinsed well, pounded to a paste	Ground nutmeg
I bunch parsley, chopped	

SICILY

Preheat oven to 350°F (175°C). Cut a "lid" from top of each tomato and reserve. Scoop out some of flesh; seed, chop and set aside. Turn tomatoes over and drain. Fry onion in a little oil; add chopped tomatoes, anchovies, parsley, capers, breadcrumbs and olives. Season with salt, pepper and a little nutmeg, if desired, and mix well. Divide between tomatoes; stuff tomatoes. Top each with reserved top slice. Put tomatoes in a baking dish, drizzle oil over them and bake for 30 minutes.　　*Photograph page 67*

CHIZZE CON FORMAGGIO ALL'EMILIANA
Parmesan cheese fritters

EMILIA-ROMAGNA

Ingredients/serves 4	¾ cup butter or solid vegetable
¼lb fresh parmesan cheese in one piece	shortening, slightly softened, diced
3½ cups all-purpose flour	Vegetable oil or solid vegetable
Pinch of baking powder	shortening for frying
Salt	Parsley

Cut the parmesan into thin slivers, or grate coarsely. Pour flour, baking powder and 1 tablespoon salt onto a board. Make a well in center and add ½ cup + 2 tablespoons butter or shortening. Rub far into flour and add enough lukewarm water to form into a dough. Knead for 10 minutes and roll out to a thin rectangular sheet. 2 inches in from edge of pastry, arrange little heaps of cheese at intervals in a row. Dot piles of cheese with remaining 2 tablespoons butter or shortening. Fold pastry over cheese and press down well with your fingers. With a pastry cutter or a knife, cut off filled strip and cut around each mound of cheese, making sure the edges are well sealed into squares or oblongs. Fry filled pastries in plenty of hot oil or shortening. Remove when golden brown and puffed up and drain on paper towels. Arrange on a serving dish, garnish with parsley and serve very hot.

SFORMATO DI FORMAGGIO
Cheese soufflé mold

EMILIA-ROMAGNA

Ingredients/serves 4	¼ lb gruyère cheese, sliced
½ cup butter	½ cup grated parmesan cheese
½ cup all-purpose flour	Salt and pepper
2½ cups hot milk	4 eggs, separated

Preheat oven to 400°F (205°C). Melt butter and gradually stir in flour. Remove from heat and gradually pour in the hot milk, still stirring, to prevent lumps forming. Stir in cheeses, season with salt and pepper and remove from heat. Pour into a bowl and allow to cool. Add egg yolks to sauce. Beat egg whites until they hold stiff peaks. Pour sauce into a greased and floured mold and fold in egg whites. Place mold in a baking dish; pour enough hot water into dish to come about 1 inch up sides of mold. Bake until set (about 30 minutes). Remove from oven and allow to stand for a few minutes before turning out onto a dish. Serve at once.

MOZZARELLA IN CAROZZA
Mozzarella in carriages

Ingredients/serves 4	2 eggs
10 slices square white bread, crusts trimmed	1-2 tablespoons whipping cream or milk
Thinly sliced mozzarella cheese	Salt
All-purpose flour	Vegetable oil or butter

CAMPANIA

Cover half the bread slices with cheese. Press the remaining bread on top. Pour cold water into a bowl and put a little flour into a second bowl. Dip each sandwich first flour, then water, holding edges firmly, and arrange on bottom of a large dish. Break eggs into a cup, beat with the cream or milk and a pinch of salt, and pour over sandwiches. Turn sandwiches over to coat completely with egg mixture. Let stand for 10 minutes. Heat some oil or butter in a skillet and brown the sandwiches on both sides. Serve very hot.

SARDINE SOTT'OLIO ALLA VENETA
Sardines with pepper and tomato sauce

Ingredients/serves 4	1 ¼ cups peeled, seeded, chopped tomatoes
12 sardines in oil	chopped tomatoes
1 green or red bell pepper, roasted skinned, cut into strips	2 tablespoons butter
	Few fresh sage leaves, chopped
Whites of 3 hard-cooked eggs, chopped	1 clove garlic, crushed
	Salt and pepper

VENETO

Bone sardines carefully and reassemble them on a serving dish. Decorate with the bell pepper and egg whites. Press tomatoes through a strainer and cream with the butter, sage and garlic. Season with salt and pepper and spoon over the sardines. *Photograph page 71*

MOUSSE DI POMODORO IN GELATINA

JELLIED TOMATO MOUSSE
For recipe, see p.63

POMODORI ALLA SICILIANA

BAKED STUFFED TOMATOES
For recipe, see p.63

PROSCIUTTO COTTO IN GELATINA
Cooked ham in gelatin

EMILIA-
ROMAGNA

Ingredients/serves 4	¹/₄ cup dry sherry
8 slices cooked ham (boiled)	1³/₄ cups beef stock
I envelope unflavored gelatin	

C ut ham slices in half and roll them up. Soften gelatin in sherry. Heat stock in a small pan; add softened gelatin and stir over low heat until completely dissolved. Pour a little gelatin into bottom of a dish and refrigerate until set. Arrange ham rolls on gelatin; drizzle remaining gelatin over ham and chill for 2 hours. The ham rolls may also be stuffed with pâté or Russian salad.

Photograph page 71

PATE DI CONIGLIO
Rabbit pâté

LAZIO, UMBRIA
AND
THE MARCHES

Ingredients/serves 12	¹/₄ cup marsala
I (4¹/₂-lb) rabbit	¹/₄ cup brandy
¹/₂ cup butter	I envelope unflavored gelatin
¹/₄ cup vegetable oil	2 cups beef stock
I clove garlic	I small black truffle (optional)
Rosemary sprig	Pickled vegetables, such
Salt and freshly ground pepper	as cauliflower, peppers, etc,
I cup dry white wine	to decorate

W ash and cut up rabbit; reserve liver. Put in a pan with I tablespoon butter, the oil, garlic and rosemary. Season with salt and pepper and cook over low heat until meat is browned all over. Pour in wine and let it evaporate a little. Reduce the heat. Cook for an hour, adding a little hot water, if necessary. Add liver 5 minutes before you take rabbit off the heat. Drain and bone rabbit pieces. Chop meat and liver and press it through a fine-meshed strainer or purée in a food processor until you have a smooth, even paste. Put in a bowl. Melt remaining 7 tablespoons butter, add to rabbit and mix with a wooden spoon. Add the marsala and brandy, sprinkle with a little freshly ground pepper and mix well. Combine gelatin and stock in a saucepan; let stand for 5 minutes, then stir over low heat until gelatin is completely dissolved. Chill until syrupy and slightly thickened. Pour a little gelatin into a rectangular mold, tipping mold to coat sides.Chill until almost set. Cut truffle (if used) and pickled vegetables into shapes with a small hors d'oeuvre cutter and arrange decoration on sides and bottom of mold. Cover with another layer of gelatin and put in refrigerator to chill and set. Cover with a further layer of gelatin. Put mold back in refrigerator. You should now have a thickish coating of gelatin. When gelatin has set, fill mold with rabbit mixture, leaving a small gap between sides and pâté. Smooth top down well.

Pour remaining gelatin into mold, letting it completely fill gaps at sides and cover top, and chill for 3-4 hours. Unmold the pâté onto a serving dish and allow to stand for 30 minutes before serving.

SUPPLI ALLA ROMANA
Roman rice croquettes

Ingredients/serves 4	
1 small onion, sliced	Few dried mushrooms
Butter	Olive oil
$\frac{1}{4}$ cup skinned, sliced sausage	About $\frac{1}{4}$ lb ground veal
1 $\frac{1}{4}$ cups peeled, seeded, chopped ripe tomatoes	Tomato paste
	Salt
1 $\frac{1}{2}$ cups rice	2 chicken livers, finely chopped
5 cups chicken or beef stock	$\frac{2}{3}$ cup diced mozzarella cheese
2 eggs, beaten	Breadcrumbs
	Solid vegetable shortening for deep-frying

LAZIO, UMBRIA
AND
THE MARCHES

L eftovers can be used to make this economical dish. Reserving a little onion, put the rest into a pan with some butter and the sausage and fry for a few minutes. Add tomatoes and cook gently for 10 minutes, stirring frequently. Add rice and pour in a ladleful of stock, adding another each time it is absorbed by rice. When rice is cooked, remove from heat and add 2 tablespoons butter and the eggs and mix well. Then turn onto a plate and cool. Meanwhile, soak mushrooms, drain and slice. Chop reserved onion slices and put in a saucepan with a little butter and oil. Then add mushrooms and veal. Dilute tomato paste in a few tablespoons water and add to pan. Season to taste with salt and cook for 30 minutes. Stir in chicken livers. Make balls or croquettes of risotto using your hands, putting a little mozzarella and veal-mushroom sauce in middle of each one. Then dip each croquette in breadcrumbs. Heat shortening in a deep skillet and deep-fry the croquettes a few at a time until golden brown. Drain on paper towels. Keep hot until all croquettes are cooked. Serve hot. When you cut the croquettes to eat them, the melted cheese inside forms long strands. The imaginative Romans call this dish "telephone cords"!

SARDINES WITH PEPPER AND TOMATO SAUCE
For recipe, see p.65

PROSCIUTTO COTTO IN GELATINA

COOKED HAM IN GELATIN
For recipe, see p.68

SOUPS

Soup would not be served in Italy at the same meal as pasta, because it often contains pasta itself. An Italian soup may be a delicate consommé garnished with dumplings or eggs, or it may be a nourishing broth thickened with rice and vegetables. Offer parmesan cheese with anything other than a fish soup.

PASSATO DI POMODORO ALLA PANNA
Creamed tomato soup

LAZIO, UMBRIA AND THE MARCHES

Ingredients/serves 4	About ½ pint whipping cream (1 cup)
4 lbs ripe tomatoes	Juice of ½ lemon
1 teaspoon sugar	½ cup chopped cooked ham
½ onion	½ cucumber, diced
Salt	1 teaspoon chopped fresh basil
1 teaspoon Worcestershire sauce	

Peel and seed tomatoes; cut into slices, then press through a strainer or purée in a blender. Pour into a pan, add sugar and chill. Slice onion, wrap in cheesecloth and squeeze juice into the tomato purée. Season with salt; add Worcestershire sauce, cream and lemon juice. Stir in ham and cucumber, sprinkle with basil and serve.

ZUPPA DI CECI ALLA CONTADINA
Country garbanzo soup

ABRUZZI-MOLISE

Ingredients/serves 4	2 tablespoons vegetable oil
1 lb dried garbanzo beans	²⁄₃ cup peeled, chopped tomatoes
¼ cup chopped pancetta bacon	
1 green onion, chopped	¾ cup chopped lean pork
1 clove garlic, sliced	Salt and pepper
1 tablespoon chopped parsley	4 slices toast
Pinch of dried leaf marjoram	½ cup grated parmesan cheese

Soak garbanzo beans in lukewarm water for 12 hours. Put pancetta, green onion, garlic, parsley and marjoram into a pan. Stir in oil, drained garbanzo beans and tomatoes; add enough water to cover. Bring to a boil. Add pork, reduce heat to medium, cover and simmer for 2 hours. Season with salt and a pinch of pepper and mix. Lay slices of toast in bottom of 4 soup bowls and pour the soup on. Pass parmesan separately.

ZUPPA DI FAGIOLI ALLA MARCHIGIANA

BEAN AND VEGETABLE SOUP
For recipe, see p.76

MINESTRA AL PESTO

VEGETABLE SOUP WITH PESTO
For recipe, see p.76

MINESTRA AL PESTO
Vegetable soup with pesto

LIGURIA

Ingredients/serves 4	½ onion, sliced
½lbs fresh spinach	2 tablespoons vegetable oil
¾ cup fresh green beans	Salt and pepper
2 potatoes, peeled, sliced	1 tablespoon pesto sauce (see
½ head green cabbage, chopped	p.48)
1 leek, sliced	¾ cup rice

W ash, trim and chop spinach. Put in a pan with beans, potatoes, cabbage, leek and onion. Stir in oil to coat. Season with salt and pepper and add 6 cups water. Bring to a boil and cook over medium heat for 1 hour. Stir in pesto, pour in rice and cook for a 15 minutes longer. Serve at once.

Photograph page 74

ZUPPA DI FAGIOLI ALLA MARCHIGIANA
Bean and vegetable soup

**LAZIO, UMBRIA
AND
THE MARCHES**

Ingredients/serves 4	1 tablespoon tomato paste
⅔ cup chopped bacon	¾ cup chopped green cabbage
1¼ cups dried white beans, soaked	¾ cup peeled, chopped potato
	½ cup cauliflowerets
Salt	1 bunch beets, cooked, peeled, diced
½ onion	
½ stalk celery	Pepper
½ bunch parsley	1¼ shelled fresh peas
Vegetable oil	4 slices toast

B lanch bacon, drain and put in a pan with beans. Pour in 7 cups water, season with salt, and cook until beans are done. Drain beans and reserve cooking liquid. Meanwhile, chop together onion, celery and parsley and fry in a large pan in a little oil until soft. Add tomato paste diluted with a little water. Pour in bean cooking liquid and stir in cabbage, potato, cauliflower and beets. Season with salt and pepper. Simmer soup for 30 minutes, adding more water if necessary. Meanwhile, purée half the beans and cook peas separately. Add all beans and peas to soup and heat through. Put toast in a soup tureen and pour in the soup. Let it stand for a few minutes before serving.

Photograph page 74

MINESTRONE ALLA MILANESE
Minestrone

LOMBARDY

Ingredients/serves 4	1 stalk celery, finely chopped
1 slice salt pork	1½ cups peeled, seeded chopped ripe tomatoes
1 lb unshelled fresh peas	2 small zucchini, finely chopped
1 lb unshelled fresh borlotti beans (see p.33) or cranberry beans	4 strips pancetta bacon, cut into ½ inch pieces
2 tablespoons parsley sprigs	Salt
1 small bunch basil	2-3 potatoes, peeled, sliced
2 fresh sage leaves	½ cup rice
1 onion	¼ head savoy cabbage, shredded
1 clove garlic	
2 strips bacon	Pepper
¼ cup butter	5 tablespoons grated parmesan cheese
1 carrot, finely chopped	

P ut salt pork into a pan of cold water and boil for 5 minutes, then plunge into cold water and let it cool. Cut into strips. Shell peas and beans and put them in separate bowls of cold water. Trim and chop parsley, basil and sage together with onion, garlic and bacon. Put herb mixture in a large pan with 2 tablespoons butter, carrot, celery, tomatoes and zucchini. Add pancetta and cook, stirring often, until onion has softened and bacon fat melted. Pour on 7½ cups boiling water, salt lightly, and bring back to a boil. Add the drained beans and pork, stir and cook for 2 hours. Add potatoes, rice, cabbage and drained peas, and cook, uncovered, until rice is al dente, stirring often. Be careful not to overcook rice, remembering it will continue to cook in the hot soup when removed from the heat. Season to taste with salt and pepper; swirl in remaining 2 tablespoons butter and 1 tablespoon parmesan. Allow to cool. Ladle into soup bowls and dust with remaining 4 tablespoons parmesan. This soup is best served cool or cold, but not chilled.

MINESTRA DI RISO E RAPE ALLA MILANESE

*R*ICE AND TURNIP SOUP
For recipe, see p.81

MALFATTINI ALLA ROMAGNOLA

Crazy-cut pasta Romagnola style
For recipe, see p.82

MINESTRONE DI VERDURA ALLA LIVORNESE
Minestrone Livorno style

TUSCANY

Ingredients/serves 4	
1 lb unshelled fresh lima beans	1¼lbs potatoes, peeled, cut into julienne strips
2 tablespoons chopped parsley	½ cup julienne-cut carrot
1 slice prosciutto	1 stalk celery, cut into julienne strips
1 clove garlic	1 zucchini, cut into julienne strips
Olive oil	1 bouillon cube
½ small head savoy cabbage, shredded	1½ cups peeled, seeded, chopped ripe tomatoes
⅔ cup trimmed, washed, shredded spinach *or* beet greens	¼ lb salt pork, blanched, cut into strips
	Salt
1 onion, chopped	⅔ cup rice
	5 tablespoons grated parmesan cheese

I n winter this can be prepared with dried soaked beans and canned tomatoes. Shell the beans and put them into cold water. Finely chop parsley, together with prosciutto and garlic. Put this in a skillet with 3 tablespoons oil. Cook for a few minutes, then add cabbage and spinach or beet greens, stir and continue to cook over medium heat. Add onion, potatoes, carrot, celery and zucchini. Pour in 5 cups water, add bouillon cube, tomatoes and salt pork. When water comes to boil, add drained beans, cover and simmer gently for 2 hours. Season to taste with salt, add rice, stir and cook, uncovered, until rice is done. The soup should be thick. Remove from heat and stir in 2 tablespoons parmesan. Serve remaining 3 tablespoons parmesan separately.

STRACCIATELLA ALLA ROMANA
Egg noodle soup

LAZIO, UMBRIA
AND
THE MARCHES

Ingredients/serves 4	
3 eggs	¼ cup grated parmesan cheese
3 tablespoons fine semolina	7½ cups beef stock
1 tablespoon chopped parsley	Salt
	Ground nutmeg

I n a bowl, beat eggs with semolina, parsley and 2 tablespoons parmesan. Pour in a cup of cold stock, season with salt and nutmeg and whisk. Bring remaining 6½ cups stock to a boil, pour in semolina mixture and stir for 3-4 minutes over medium heat until fine shreds of egg form in the soup. Serve at once, sprinkled with remaining 2 tablespoons parmesan.

MINESTRA DI RISO E RAPE ALLA MILANESE
Rice and turnip soup

Ingredients/serves 4	2 medium turnips, peeled,
2 tablespoons parsley sprigs	thinly sliced
2 strips bacon *or*	5 ½ cups beef stock
pancetta bacon	¾ cup rice
Butter	6 tablespoons grated parmesan
	cheese

LOMBARDY

Finely chop parsely together with bacon. Fry for a few minutes in a little butter. Then add turnips and cook for a few more minutes. Add stock, bring to a boil and simmer for 7 minutes. Add rice, stir and cook, uncovered, until just al dente. A minute before removing from heat, stir in 2 tablespoons parmesan, then serve, passing remaining 4 tablespoons cheese separately. If turnips are very young and tender you can add them when you put in rice.

Photograph page 78

MINESTRA DI PASTA ALL'UOVO E PISELLI
Egg pasta and pea soup

Ingredients/serves 4	1 tablespoon tomato paste
½ carrot, chopped	Salt and pepper
½ onion, chopped	¾ cup shelled young, fresh peas
½ stalk celery, chopped	(petits pois)
1 tablespoon chopped parsley	¾ cup small egg pasta shapes
2 tablespoons butter	½ cup grated parmesan cheese

VENETO

Gently fry carrot, onion, celery and parsley in a pan with butter until golden brown. Add tomato paste diluted with 2 tablespoons water, season with salt and pepper and cook for 10 minutes. Pour in 6 cups water, bring to a boil and add peas. Cook for 25 minutes, add pasta and cook for a further 15 minutes. Serve at once, passing cheese separately.

MALFATTINI ALLA ROMAGNOLA
Crazy-cut pasta Romagnola style

EMILIA-
ROMAGNA

Ingredients/serves 4	Salt
1 ¼ cups all-purpose flour	Pinch of ground nutmeg
3 eggs, beaten	1 ½ quarts chicken or beef stock

H eap flour on work surface, make a well in the middle and add eggs and a pinch of salt and nutmeg. Form into a dough and knead mixture until it is smooth. Form dough into a rectangular loaf shape and leave to dry out a little. Cut it into thick slices and let dry a little longer. Chop coarsely and dry out completely. Pour stock into a pan and bring to the boil. Add pasta and cook for 2-3 minutes, then serve in soup bowls. *Photograph page 79*

TIELLA ALLA PUGLIESE
Mussel and potato soup

APULIA

Ingredients/serves 4	½ small onion
1 ½ lbs mussels	1 clove garlic
Vegetable oil	1 ¼ cups peeled, sliced potatoes
Freshly ground black pepper	Salt
2 strips bacon	¾ cup rice

P ull off and discard beards from mussels; rinse mussels well under cold running water. Cook in a large pan over low heat with a little oil and a pinch of freshly ground pepper until they open. Drain, reserving liquid discard any mussels that remain closed. Remove the mussels from their shells. Chop bacon, onion and garlic finely together and put into a pan with 1 tablespoon oil. Pour in 5¼ cups water, add potatoes, season with salt and bring to a boil. Simmer for 10 minutes, then add the rice and cook briskly. Just before soup is cooked, strain reserved mussel cooking liquid and add to soup with mussels. Heat through for a couple of minutes and serve. *Photograph page 85*

CACCIUCCO
Tuscan fish soup

TUSCANY

Ingredients/serves 4	I large onion, thinly sliced
2lbs assorted fresh whole fish, large and small	I stalk celery, thinly sliced
	I carrot, thinly sliced
I ¼lbs assorted seafood, including squid, shrimp etc	Salt and pepper
	½ cup dry white wine
I ¾cups mussels *or* clams	3 medium ripe tomatoes, peeled, seeded, sliced
¼ cup parsley sprigs	
3 cloves garlic	4 large *or* 8 small slices firm white bread
I red chili pepper	
Olive oil	

T his delicious fish soup can easily be a main course in itself. Any seafood can be used: mullet, eel, shrimp, crayfish etc, provided it is very fresh. Clean fish, keeping heads to one side, leaving small fish whole and cutting big ones into equal-size chunks. Wash and drain well. Clean and prepare squid; shell and devein shrimps. Then clean mussels or clams, washing very well. Soaking for a couple of hours helps to get rid of any sand. Wash and trim the parsley and chop it together with 2 cloves garlic and the chili pepper. Put this mixture with ¼ cup oil into a large saucepan over medium heat. Add onion, celery and carrot, season with salt and pepper and fry gently, stirring well. Then add seafood and fish and cook gently, gradually stirring in wine. When wine has evaporated, add mussels or clams. When they have opened, remove and reserve. Add tomatoes and continue cooking until squid is done, adding a little water, if necessary. Meanwhile, poach fish heads separately in water for about 15-20 minutes. Discard bones; push flesh through a strainer or purée in a blender. Stir purée into soup. If mixture is very thick, add a little boiling water. Season to taste. Preheat oven to 370°F (190°C). Rub bread with remaining I clove garlic and put on a baking sheet in oven. When bread has hardened, lay slices in a large tureen or in individual soup bowls. When soup is done, remove bones if you wish, correct seasoning and pour over bread. Serve immediately, accompanied by same wine used for cooking.

Photograph page 84

CACCIUCCO

TUSCAN FISH SOUP
For recipe, see p.83

TIELLA ALLA PUGLIESE

MUSSEL AND POTATO SOUP
For recipe, see p.82

PASTA

Pasta is traditionally made at home in central and northern Italy, and produced in factories and sold in packages in the south. Now, with more women out at work, both fresh and dried pasta are readily available in the shops, but there is still nothing quite like making it yourself.

SPAGHETTI AGLIO E OLIO
Spaghetti with garlic and oil

Ingredients/serves 4	
1 lb spaghetti	1 red chili pepper
1/3 cup virgin olive oil	5 tablespoons chopped parsley
3 cloves garlic	Freshly ground pepper

CAMPANIA

F or this Neapolitan dish you should use the very best olive oil. Bring a large pan of salted water to a boil and cook pasta until al dente. Halfway through pasta cooking time, heat oil in a pan and add the whole garlic and chili pepper. Fry until garlic has turned golden, then remove garlic and chili. Drain pasta. Pour into a bowl. Add parsley to the oil, pour it into bowl onto spaghetti, add freshly ground pepper and serve immediately.

SPAGHETTI ALLA PUTTANESCA
Spaghetti with hot sauce

Ingredients/serves 4	
2/3 cup ripe olives	1/3 cup olive oil
4 or 5 flat anchovy fillets	2 cloves garlic, crushed
1 lb ripe tomatoes	1 red chili pepper, chopped
1 tablespoon capers	1 tablespoon tomato paste
	12 oz spaghetti

CAMPANIA

P ut on a pan of salted water to boil for pasta. Pit olives; rinse anchovies well in cold water. Peel, seed and chop tomatoes. Wash capers thoroughly to eliminate of excess saltiness. Put oil into a pan with garlic, chili and anchovies and fry, stirring. Add tomatoes, tomato paste, capers and olives and cook briskly for a few minutes, stirring often. Cook spaghetti in boiling water until al dente, drain, stir in the sauce and serve. *Photograph page 89*

SPAGHETTI CON LE VONGOLE

SPAGHETTI WITH CLAMS
For recipe, see p.90

SPAGHETTI ALLA PUTTANESCA

SPAGHETTI WITH HOT SAUCE
For recipe, see p.87

SPAGHETTI CON LE VONGOLE
Spaghetti with clams

CAMPANIA

Ingredients/serves 4	¼ cup olive oil
2½ lbs clams	Pepper
2½ lbs ripe tomatoes	1 lb spaghetti *or* trenette
2 cloves garlic, crushed	2 tablespoons chopped parsley

Wash clams thoroughly, rinsing away any sand. If possible, let soak in cold salted water for 1-2 hours. Put them in a large pan, cover and cook over low heat, shaking occasionally, until all clams are open. Remove clams from their shells and transfer to a bowl. If they still seem to have sand in them when cooked, rinse in lukewarm water. Strain clam cooking liquid through cheesecloth and set aside. Peel and seed tomatoes, then chop or press through a strainer, if you prefer. Fry crushed garlic in oil until lightly browned. Add tomatoes, clam liquid and a pinch of pepper and cook over high heat, stirring often. Cook spaghetti or trenette in plenty of boiling salted water until al dente. A minute before pasta is done, add clams and parsley to tomato mixture, bring to boil and remove from heat immediately. Drain pasta, transfer to a serving dish, mix in sauce and serve. *Photograph page 89*

SPAGHETTI ALLA CARBONARA
Spaghetti with bacon and eggs

LAZIO, UMBRIA
AND
THE MARCHES

Ingredients/serves 4-5	¼ cup whipping cream
½ cup diced pancetta bacon	Pepper
¼ cup butter	1 lb spaghetti
4 eggs	⅓ cup grated parmesan cheese

Fry the pancetta in butter, remove with a slotted spoon and keep hot. Beat eggs in a large bowl with cream and a pinch of pepper. Cook spaghetti al dente in plenty of boiling salted water, drain, pour into a bowl with the eggs and mix well. Sprinkle with the pancetta and parmesan and serve at once.

VERMICELLI PICCANTI ALLA CALABRESE
Spicy vermicelli

CALABRIA

Ingredients/serves 4	Vegetable oil
I lb vermicelli	2 red chili peppers, chopped
8 flat anchovy fillets	I tablespoon chopped parsley
I clove garlic, chopped	

Boil vermicelli in plenty of salted water until al dente, drain and put on a serving dish. Meanwhile, prepare sauce. Thoroughly rinse anchovies and pound in a mortar. Fry garlic in oil until soft. Add the chili peppers, anchovies and parsley. Pour sauce on the vermicelli and serve.

RAVIOLI ALLA SALVIA CON LA ZUCCA
Ravioli with sage and pumpkin

LIGURIA

Ingredients/serves 4	Coarse-grained mustard, or
For the pasta	Italian fruity mustard, if
3 $\frac{1}{2}$ cups all-purpose flour	available
Salt	Salt and pepper
5 eggs	Pinch of ground nutmeg
I teaspoon vegetable oil	*For the sauce*
For the filling	$\frac{1}{2}$ cup melted, browned butter
4 $\frac{1}{4}$ lbs pumpkin, seeded	Few fresh sage leaves, chopped
$\frac{1}{2}$ cup grated parmesan cheese	$\frac{1}{3}$ cup grated parmesan cheese
4 crushed amaretti biscuits	

Preheat oven to 400°F (200°C). *For the pasta,* follow instructions on pp.51-52, mixing a pinch of salt with the flour. *For the filling,* bake pumpkin until tender and scrape flesh into a bowl. Mash pumpkin well. Stir in parmesan, amaretti cookies, and the mustard. Season with salt, pepper and a pinch of nutmeg and mix well. *To prepare ravioli,* make according to instructions on p. 55, placing filling at 2-2$\frac{1}{2}$-inch intervals. Boil ravioli in plenty of salted water until al dente. Drain and arrange in layers in a baking dish, topping each layer with melted, browned butter, sage and parmesan. Finish with a sprinkling of parmesan. Bake in oven until golden brown. *Photograph page 92*

RAVIOLI ALLA SALVIA CON LA ZUCCA

*R*AVIOLI WITH SAGE AND PUMPKIN
For recipe, see p.91

PASTICCIO DI TORTELLINI ALLA BOLOGNESE

BOLOGNESE TORTELLINI PIE
For recipe, see p.96

RAVIOLI CON LA RICOTTA
Ravioli with ricotta

LAZIO, UMBRIA
AND
THE MARCHES

Ingredients/serves 4	¼ cup grated parmesan cheese
For the pasta	I egg and I egg yolk
1¾ cups all-purpose flour	Salt and pepper
I tablespoon vegetable oil	*To serve*
4 eggs and a little water, *or* 5 eggs	2-4 tablespoons melted, browned butter
Salt	Fresh sage leaves, chopped
For the filling	Grated parmesan cheese
I lb ricotta cheese	

Pour flour into a mound on the work surface. Make a well in center and add oil, eggs and a pinch of salt. Work ingredients together, adding a little water if you are using 4 eggs, to make dough. Knead until pliable. Allow dough to rest for 30 minutes. Combine ingredients for filling. Roll out dough and prepare ravioli as on pp.52 and 55. Boil in plenty of salted water until al dente. Transfer to a hot serving dish and pour over melted, browned butter. Sprinkle with fresh sage and plenty of parmesan to serve. The ravioli can also be served with a tomato sauce flavored with a little basil.

MACCHERONCINI CON I GAMBERI
Macaroni with shrimp

VENETO

Ingredients/serves 4	I lb macaroni
I teaspoon dried leaf thyme	2 cloves garlic, crushed
I bay leaf	Vegetable oil
2 tablespoons chopped parsley	I red chili pepper, chopped
Salt	1¾ cups peeled, chopped tomatoes
1½ cups uncooked shrimp, unshelled	

Put thyme, bay leaf, I tablespoon parsley and a pinch of salt into a pan of water, bring to boil and add shrimp. Cook for 3 minutes, then drain. Shell, devein and coarsley chop shrimp. Cook macaroni in plenty of boiling salted water until al dente. Fry garlic in oil, add chili pepper and tomatoes, season with salt and cook for 10 minutes. Add shrimp. Drain pasta, mix in sauce and sprinkle on remaining I tablespoon chopped parsley.

RAVIOLI ALLA PANNA GRATINATI
Gratin of ravioli with cream

EMILIA-
ROMAGNA

Ingredients/serves 4	2 tablespoons breadcrumbs
For the pasta	Salt and pepper
1¾ cups all-purpose flour	2 egg yolks
Salt	2 tablespoons grated parmesan
5 eggs	cheese
1 tablespoon oil	*For the sauce*
For the filling	½ cup butter
2 tablespoons chopped onion	5 tablespoons grated parmesan
3 tablespoons butter	cheese
1½ cups finely diced sausage	About ½ pint half-and-half (1 cup)

Preheat oven to 400°F (205°C). *For the pasta*, follow instructions on pp.51-52, mixing a pinch of salt with the flour. *For the filling*, soften onion in butter, add sausage, breadcrumbs, salt and pepper and cook gently for 10 minutes. Transfer the sauce to a bowl and allow it to cool. Mix in egg yolks and parmesan. Assemble ravioli according to instructions on p.55. Boil ravioli in plenty of salted water for about 7 minutes or until they rise to surface of water and lose their pasty appearance. Drain and arrange in a baking dish in layers; dot each layer with butter, sprinkle with parmesan and drizzle with half-and-half. Bake until golden brown.

BUCATINI ALL'AMATRICIANA
Bucatini with bacon and tomatoes

LAZIO, UMBRIA
AND
THE MARCHES

Ingredients/serves 4	Salt and white pepper
½ cup chopped pancetta bacon	1 lb bucatini (or other
2 tablespoons solid vegetable	pasta shapes)
shortening	¼ cup grated pecorino cheese
1 small onion, finely chopped	
2 cups peeled, seeded, chopped	
firm-ripe tomatoes	

Put on plenty of salted water to boil for pasta. Put pancetta in a saucepan with shortening and onion and fry until bacon is browned. Add tomatoes, season lightly with salt and white pepper and cook briskly for about 10 minutes. Meanwhile, cook pasta until al dente, drain, transfer to bowl, add cheese and sauce, stir and serve hot.

PASTICCIO DI TORTELLINI ALLA BOLOGNESE

Bolognese tortellini pie

EMILIA-
ROMAGNA

Ingredients/serves 4	I whole clove
For the filling	I bay leaf
$\frac{1}{4}$ cup butter	Salt and pepper
I $\frac{1}{4}$ cups chopped sausage	About $\frac{1}{2}$ pint whipping cream
$\frac{1}{2}$ cup chopped mortadella	(I cup)
$\frac{2}{3}$ cup chopped turkey breast	4-5 chicken livers
$\frac{1}{2}$ cup chopped prosciutto	*For the pasta*
I egg	I $\frac{3}{4}$ cups all-purpose flour
6 tablespoons grated parmesan cheese	4 eggs
Pinch of ground nutmeg	*For the pastry*
Salt and pepper	I $\frac{1}{4}$ cups flour
For the sauce	Salt
I carrot	Pinch of sugar
I onion	$\frac{2}{3}$ cup butter, softened, cut into
I stalk celery	small pieces
$\frac{1}{2}$ cup chopped pancetta bacon	I egg yolk
$\frac{3}{4}$ cup finely chopped lean, boneless pork	1-2 tablespoons dry white wine
About $\frac{1}{2}$ lb lean ground beef	Grated lemon peel (optional)
$\frac{1}{2}$ cup finely chopped prosciutto	*To assemble*
$\frac{1}{4}$ cup butter	$\frac{1}{4}$ cup butter
2 tablespoons tomato sauce	6 tablespoons grated parmesan cheese
	Breadcrumbs

I t is recommended that you prepare the filling for the pasta and the sauce I or 2 days ahead of time and the pastry on the next day, as there is a fair amount of work involved. Put the pasticcio together on the day you want to serve it. *For the filling,* melt butter in a pan. Add sausages, turkey and prosciutto and cook gently, stirring. Remove from heat. Stir in the egg, parmesan and nutmeg; season with salt and pepper. Use to fill the tortellini. *For the sauce,* prepare and then chop together carrot, onion and celery; place chopped vegetables and pancetta in a pan with pork, beef and prosciutto. Fry gently with butter, stirring until vegetables have softened and meat has changed color. Add tomato sauce diluted in water, clove and bay leaf. Season with salt and pepper, stir and cook very gently for an hour, adding cream when sauce starts to dry out. Five minutes before end of cooking time, wash chicken livers thoroughly and chop them. Add to sauce. *For the pasta,* follow instructions on pp. 51-52. Let dough rest, then make tortellini as directed on p. 56. *For the pastry,* pour flour onto a board, make a well in the center and put in a pinch of salt, sugar, butter, egg yolk and white wine (plus a little grated lemon peel, if desired). Mix together with fingertips, but do not work longer than necessary. Roll into a ball, wrap and chill for an hour, or overnight if preferred. *To assemble pasticcio,* bring a pan of salted water to a boil and cook tortellini, removing them while still very al dente. Transfer them to a bowl, add sauce, 3 tablespoons butter and 6 tablespoons parmesan and mix well. Allow to cool. Grease a deep cake pan (with removable sides if possible); dust with breadcrumbs, shaking out excess. Preheat oven to 350°F (180°C). Remove pastry from fridge and cut into two pieces, one twice as big as the other. Roll out bigger piece into a circle large enough to line cake pan and put it in. Fill with tortellini and dot with remaining 1 tablespoon butter. Roll out a circle of pastry to cover pasticcio, press it on at edges, dampening them first, and decorate with pastry trimmings (diamonds, hearts, half-moons etc). Prick with a fork and bake for about 40 minutes. Let pasticcio stand for 10 minutes before cutting and serving.

Photograph page 93

RICCHIE I PRIVIETI ALLA CALABRESE
Ricchie with meat and pecorino sauce

CALABRIA

Ingredients/serves 4	For the sauce
For the pasta	2 cups tomato and meat sauce (see p.47)
1 ¾ cups all-purpose flour	⅓ cup grated pecorino cheese
Pinch of salt	
4 eggs	
1 teaspoon vegetable oil	
or 14 oz ricchie (pasta shaped like little ears)	

E ither buy ready-made ricchie, or make fresh pasta with ingredients given, following instructions pp. 51-52. Let dough rest for 30 minutes, then roll it out and cut into little discs. With a floured thumb, press each disc into the shape of an ear. Allow to dry. Boil ricchie in plenty of salted water until al dente. Drain and mix in hot tomato and meat sauce and a few tablespoons pecorino. Serve remaining cheese separately.

Photograph page 101

ZITE RIPIENI STUFATE ALLA CASERTANA

Stuffed braised zite

CAMPANIA

Ingredients/serves 4	Ground nutmeg
I teaspoon chopped onion	2 eggs, beaten
$\frac{1}{3}$ cup pork kidney fat *or* lard	I lb zite (big macaroni)
About Ilb lean ground pork	I teaspoon breadcrumbs
$\frac{1}{2}$ cup skinned, finely chopped or ground salami	2 cups fresh tomato sauce
	$\frac{1}{3}$ cup grated caciocavallo
Salt and pepper	cheese

Preheat oven to 400°F (205°C). Fry onion in half the kidney fat or lard; add the pork and salami. Season with salt and pepper, add a pinch of nutmeg and cook for 20 minutes. Remove from heat, allow to cool and stir in eggs. Boil zite in plenty of salted water until al dente. Drain and allow to cool, then fill with stuffing. Grease a casserole dish with remaining kidney fat or lard and sprinkle with breadcrumbs. Arrange the stuffed zite in layers with the tomato sauce and the cheese. Bake for 20-30 minutes or until golden brown on top. Serve at once. *Photograph page 101*

CAPPELLETTI CON RIPIENO

Cappelletti with chicken stuffing

EMILIA-ROMAGNA

Ingredients/serves 4	$\frac{2}{3}$ cup shredded mascarpone
For the pasta	cheese
I cup all-purpose flour	I egg
2 eggs	7 tablespoons grated parmesan
For the filling and sauce	cheese
$\frac{1}{4}$ cup chopped prosciutto	Salt and pepper
$\frac{1}{2}$ cup butter	I teaspoon all-purpose flour
$\frac{1}{2}$ lb skinned, boned chicken breast	Scant teaspoon browning sauce
	About $\frac{1}{2}$ pint whipping cream
Good-quality cognac	(I cup)

Put prosciutto in a small pan with 2 tablespoons butter and fry for I minute. Add chicken and a little cognac and cook over low heat without letting meat brown. Meanwhile, pour flour onto a board and make a well in center. Break eggs into it and mix together well. Put dough into a plastic bag and close it tightly. When chicken is cooked, remove it from pan and chop very finely. Put into a bowl; add cooking juices, mascarpone, egg and half the parmesan. Season with salt and pepper and stir well. Roll out pasta and make cappelletti (see pp. 51-52, 54), stuffing them with the chicken filling. Put cappelletti on a floured tray, not letting them touch. Bring a large pan of salted water to a boil. Blend flour and browning sauce into cream without letting lumps form. Melt remaining 6 table-spoons butter in a small pan, then add cream mixture. Let boil, stirring, for 2 minutes, then set aside and keep warm. Boil cappelletti in salted water and remove with a slotted spoon. Put a layer of pasta into a dish, pour on some cream sauce, sprinkle with some of remaining parmesan, add another layer of cappel-letti, a layer of sauce and so on until all ingredients have been used. Serve hot.

TORTELLONI CON PASTA VERDE AL GRATIN
Spinach tortelloni bake

LAZIO, UMBRIA AND THE MARCHES

Ingredients/serves 4	1 egg yolk
For the pasta	Pinch of ground nutmeg
1¾ cups all-purpose flour	Salt and pepper
½ lb fresh spinach, cooked, puréed, thoroughly drained	For the sauce
	1 small onion, chopped
4 eggs	2 tablespoons olive oil
For the filling	1½ cups sieved tomatoes
1½ cups ricotta cheese	Chopped fresh basil leaves
1 lb fresh spinach, cooked, puréed, thoroughly drained	Salt and pepper
	¼ cup butter
½ cup chopped prosciutto	3 tablespoons grated parmesan cheese
3 tablespoons grated parmesan cheese	Sliced mozzarella cheese

For the pasta, follow instructions on pp. 51-52. For the filling, thoroughly mix all filling ingredients together. Cut out the pasta, fill and shape into tor-telloni (see illustrations 1 and 2 on p.56). For the sauce, cook onion in oil until softened, stir in tomatoes and basil leaves and season with salt and pepper. Cook the tortelloni in boiling salted water until al dente. Layer the tortelloni in a buttered baking dish; dot each layer with butter, sprinkle with parmesan and spread with tomato sauce. Finish with a layer of mozzarella cheese and put into a hot oven until the cheese melts. Serve hot.   *Photograph page 56*

Ricchie WITH MEAT AND PECORINO SAUCE
For recipe, see p.97

ZITE RIPIENI STUFATE ALLA CASERTANA

Stuffed braised zite
For recipe, see p.98

PRIMI PIATTI

The "first course" in Italy might be soup, rice or pasta, or it might be any of the following dishes, notably gnocchi or polenta — simple, sustaining foods that cost very little. Made with care and imagination, these dishes form the basis of a characteristic Italian meal.

PAPPA COL POMODORO
Thick tomato soup

Ingredients/serves 4	1 cup cubed slightly stale bread
1 ¾ lbs ripe tomatoes	(about 2 days old)
¼ cup virgin olive oil	Salt and pepper
3 cloves garlic, crushed	5 cups beef stock
Few fresh sage and basil leaves	

TUSCANY

Wash and peel tomatoes. Remove seeds from half the tomatoes; press other half through a strainer. Heat oil in a pan and add crushed garlic, sage and basil. Cook for 1-2 minutes, then add bread and fry all over until golden brown. Add all tomatoes, season with salt and pepper and cook for 10 minutes, stirring. Gradually add stock and cook until you have a thick, soupy consistency. It can be served hot, warm or cooled, but do not refrigerate.

SPIEDINI DI FONTINA
Fontina kabobs

Ingredients/serves 4	½ cup all-purpose flour
10 oz fontina cheese	1 egg
¼ lb smoked pancetta bacon	Salt
8 square slices of bread	¾ cup breadcrumbs
2 egg yolks	Vegetable oil
1 cup hot béchamel sauce	
Pepper	

LAZIO, UMBRIA AND THE MARCHES

Cut fontina and the pancetta into 20 cubes each. Remove crusts from bread and cut each slice into quarters. Onto 4 skewers put 5 cubes of cheese, alternating with 8 quarter-slices of bread and 5 cubes of pancetta. Add 2 egg yolks to hot béchamel with a pinch of pepper and dip skewers into it to coat. Allow to cool, then dip in flour. Beat egg with a pinch of salt and dip kabobs in that and finally into breadcrumbs. Fry in hot oil until golden brown. Drain on paper towels, put on a dish and serve.

TORTA PASQUALINA

SORREL AND EGG PIE
For recipe, see p.107

PUCCIA ALLA PIEMONTESE

*P*OLENTA WITH PORK AND CABBAGE
For recipe, see p.106

PUCCIA ALLA PIEMONTESE
Polenta with pork and cabbage

PIEDMONT

Ingredients/serves 4	1 onion, cut into chunks
1 ¼ cups yellow cornmeal	1 carrot, cut into chunks
2 tablespoons all-purpose flour	1 stalk celery, cut into chunks
6 cups water	Salt and pepper
Salt	⅔ cup butter, diced
1 head savoy cabbage	½ cup grated parmesan cheese
1 ½ lbs lean, boneless pork	

Prepare polenta with cornmeal, flour, water and salt according to instructions on p. 59. Remove tough outer leaves and stalks from cabbage, cut into quarters, and boil in salted water. Drain and set aside. Put pork in a heavy saucepan, cover with cold water, bring to boil and add the onion, carrot and celery. Season with salt and pepper and simmer until just cooked. Transfer meat to a plate and cut into cubes. Pour stock through a fine strainer. Pour 1 cup strained stock back into pan and add meat and cabbage. Add prepared polenta and mix well. Remove from heat, stir in butter and parmesan and mix well. Serve in soup plates. *Photograph page 105*

POLENTA TARAGNA
Buckwheat polenta

VENETO

Ingredients/serves 4	⅔ cup yellow cornmeal
¾ cup buckwheat flour	½ cup butter, diced
Salt	¼ lb jack cheese, sliced

Pour buckwheat flour into a large saucepan and gradually add 5 cups cold water, stirring continuously so as not to let lumps form. Add a pinch of salt, put pan over medium heat and bring mixture to a boil, stirring constantly. When it begins to boil, add cornmeal. Continue to cook, stirring, for 30 minutes; add butter and cook for 20 minutes longer, still stirring. Then add cheese, cook until melted and pour polenta onto a serving dish. The cheese should be well mixed in so that you can see strands of white cheese against darker polenta. *Photograph page 108*

TORTA PASQUALINA
Sorrel and egg pie

Ingredients/serves 4	
4 ⅓ cups all-purpose flour	½ cup grated parmesan cheese
Vegetable oil	Dried leaf marjoram
Salt	9 eggs
2 lbs sorrel	Pepper
	1 ¾ cups ricotta cheese

LIGURIA

P our flour onto a board and make a well in the center. Mix in 2 tablespoons oil, a pinch of salt and enough lukewarm water to give a dough of same consistency as for homemade pasta (see p. 51). Knead for 10 minutes. Divide into 14 pieces and shape each one into a ball. Dust with flour, cover and let stand for an hour. Preheat oven to 400°F (205°C). Wash sorrel, discarding any discolored leaves and large stalks. Put it in a pan with only the water clinging to it, cover and cook gently over low heat, stirring occasionally to make sure it does not stick to pan. When sorrel is cooked (about 8 minutes), squeeze out water, then chop sorrel and place in a bowl. Add ¼ cup parmesan, a pinch of marjoram, 3 eggs and the ricotta. Season mixture with salt and pepper, then mix well. Roll out one of pastry balls very thinly and lay on a greased baking sheet. Sprinkle it with a few drops of oil. Roll out second pastry ball and lay it on top of the first. Continue rolling, oiling and stacking the pastry balls until you have 7 layers. Put sorrel filling on top. Make 6 dents with back of a spoon and into each break an egg. Season and sprinkle with remaining ¼ cup parmesan. Roll out other 7 balls until very thin and lay them on top, greasing each one with oil. Prick top sheet with a fork, brush with a little oil and bake in oven for an hour. Allow to cool and serve cold.

Photograph page 104

FRITTATA DI SCALOGNI
Shallot omelet

Ingredients/serves 4	
1 lb shallots	6 eggs
All-purpose flour	Salt and pepper
3 tablespoons vegetable oil	½ teaspoon dried leaf thyme

BASILICATA

P eel shallots, boil until tender and drain. Dust lightly with flour and fry in oil. Beat eggs in a bowl with a pinch of salt, pepper and thyme. Add them to shallots in skillet; stir with a wooden spoon and shake gently to prevent mixture from sticking to the bottom. When it has started to set, invert omelet, using a plate; slide back into skillet and cook on other side. Serve very hot.

Photograph page 109

POLENTA TARAGNA

Buckwheat polenta
For recipe, see p.106

FRITTATA DI SCALOGNI

SHALLOT OMELET
For recipe, see p.107

GNOCCHI AL GORGONZOLA
Gnocchi with gorgonzola

VENETO

Ingredients/serves 4	For the sauce
For the gnocchi	¼ cup crumbled mild
1¼ lbs russet potatoes	gorgonzola cheese
1¼ cups all-	½ cup butter
purpose flour	Pepper
1 egg	3 tablespoons grated
1 tablespoon grappa	parmesan cheese
1 teaspoon salt	¼ cup whipping cream, warmed

Prepare gnocchi according to instructions on pp. 57-58. Bring a pan of salted water to a boil and warm a bowl. Put gorgonzola into bowl with butter and a pinch of pepper and blend until creamy with a wooden spoon. Stir in parmesan and heated cream. Keep warm. Add gnocchi carefully to boiling water. Stir and cook briskly. When they come to surface, remove with a slotted spoon and transfer to bowl with the sauce. Stir well to coat with sauce and serve immediately.

GNOCCHI ALLA BAVA
Gnocchi with cheese

EMILIA-
ROMAGNA

Ingredients/serves 4	For the sauce
For the gnocchi	⅔ cup butter, melted
1¼ lbs russet	1¼ cups diced fontina cheese
potatoes	6 tablespoons grated
1 cup all-purpose flour	parmesan cheese
1 teaspoon salt	

Prepare gnocchi according to instructions on pp. 57-58. Bring a pan of salted water to a boil. Add gnocchi carefully and cook over a high heat. As gnocchi come to surface, remove with a slotted spoon. Arrange them in layers in a heated bowl, topping each layer with melted butter, fontina and parmesan. Put bowl over pan of boiling gnocchi water (without letting any water in) for about 10 minutes or until the cheese melts. Serve very hot.

UOVA IN CAMICIA CON PEPERONI
Poached eggs with red peppers

VENETO

Ingredients/serves 4	1 tablespoon vinegar
4 red bell peppers	8 eggs
Vegetable oil	2 tablespoons grated
Salt	parmesan cheese
8 strips lean pancetta bacon	¼ cup butter, melted

P reheat oven to 425°F (220°C). Bake peppers until slightly charred. Reduce oven temperature to 400°F (205°C). Peel, seed and slice peppers, then season with a little oil and salt. Blanch pancetta and then fry for a few minutes with peppers in a little oil. Bring a wide, deep pan of salted water to a boil add vinegar. Break eggs one by one into a saucer, slide them into water and when whites have set, drain and plunge into cold water. Grease a dish and arrange pancetta on bottom. Arrange eggs and peppers on top and sprinkle with parmesan. Pour over melted butter, bake for 5 minutes and serve.

BUDINO DI SALMONE
Salmon loaf

LAZIO, UMBRIA
AND
THE MARCHES

Ingredients/serves 4	1 tablespoon butter
1 ¼ lbs salmon	2 tablespoons chopped parsley
1 small carrot, cut into chunks	Salt and pepper
1 onion, cut into chunks	3 eggs
1 stalk celery, cut into chunks	⅔ cup milk
Whole black peppercorns	1 tablespoon all-purpose flour
4 medium potatoes	

P reheat oven to 350°F (175°C). Poach salmon in a pan of water, with carrot, onion, celery and a few peppercorns. Lift out salmon; cut into strips, discarding bones. Boil unpeeled potatoes separately in salted water until cooked. Peel and slice. Butter a casserole dish and put in alternating layers of potato and the salmon. Sprinkle each layer with parsley, salt and pepper. Beat eggs with milk and flour and pour over mixture. Bake for 30 minutes or until the top is golden brown. Serve at once.

PIZZA ALLA NAPOLETANA
Neapolitan pizza

CAMPANIA

Ingredients/serves 4	Sliced or diced mozzarella cheese
3 medium firm-ripe tomatoes	Dried leaf oregano
1 recipe pizza dough (see p. 60)	Coarse salt
Flat anchovy fillets	2 tablespoons olive oil

Preheat oven to 475°F (245°C). Peel and seed tomatoes, then chop. Roll out pizza dough and lay on an oiled baking sheet. Arrange anchovies, tomatoes and mozzarella on top. Sprinkle with oregano and salt, drizzle with olive oil and bake for 15 minutes.

PIZZA FANTASIA
Fancy pizza

CAMPANIA

Ingredients/serves 4	12 pitted green olives
1 recipe pizza dough (see p. 60)	1 tablespoon capers
	4 small pickles
1¾ cups peeled, chopped tomatoes	Marinated artichoke hearts, drained, sliced
Finely diced mozzarella cheese	Pepper
8 flat anchovy fillets, chopped	¼ cup olive oil

Preheat oven to 475°F (245°C). Roll out dough into a circle, put on an oiled baking sheet and cover with tomatoes. Arrange mozzarella, anchovies, olives, capers, pickles and artichokes on top. Sprinkle with pepper and drizzle with oil. Bake for 15 minutes. *Photograph page 115*

PIZZA TOPPINGS

Topping for pizza marinara

3 medium firm-ripe toma-toes (not watery)
2-3 cloves garlic
Dried leaf oregano
Olive oil
Coarse salt

Topping for pizza 4 stagioni

Cooked clams
Cooked mussels
Pitted ripe olives cut into pieces
Flat anchovy fillets
Marinated artichoke hearts

Topping for pizza Margherita

Thin slivers of mozzarella cheese
Tomatoes
Shredded fresh basil
Grated pecorino cheese
Salt
Olive oil

Other suggested toppings:

Capers
Chopped pitted ripe olives
Chopped pitted green olives
Marinated mushrooms
Roasted peppers cut into strips

Seafood (add near the end of cooking time)
Flaked tuna
Sliced cooked ham
Cubed salami
Sliced pancetta bacon
Sliced sausage

Cubed fontina cheese
Gruyère, gorgonzola, gouda cheeses (grated or sliced)
Sliced hard-cooked eggs
Fresh or dried basil, marjoram, parsley

PIZZETTE CON LE ALICI

Individual pizzas with anchovies

Ingredients/serves 4	2 cloves garlic, crushed
2 lbs fresh anchovies	2 tablespoons chopped parsley
1 recipe pizza dough (see p. 60)	Olive oil
Pepper and salt	

CAMPANIA

P reheat oven to 475°F (245°C). Remove heads from anchovies, wash and dry well. Use canned anchovies if fresh ones are not available. Roll dough into 4 thin circles and put on a greased baking sheet. Arrange anchovies on pizzas and season with pepper and a little salt. Sprinkle anchovies with garlic and parsley and moisten with a few spoonfuls of oil. Bake for 30 minutes and serve at once.

Photograph page 115

PIZZETTE CON LE ALICI

INDIVIDUAL PIZZAS WITH ANCHOVIES
For recipe, see p.113

PIZZA FANTASIA

FANCY PIZZA
For recipe, see p.112

RICE

An Italian risotto is tender and moist, not dry, unlike the rice dishes of India and the Middle East. Serve it in soup plates, sprinkled with plenty of parmesan cheese.

RISOTTO ALLA SBIRRAGLIA
Chicken risotto

Ingredients/serves 4	Salt
1 (about 3-lb) broiler-fryer, cooked, giblets reserved	½ cups butter
⅔ cup chopped veal	Pepper
1 carrot, chopped	1 cup dry white wine
1 onion, chopped	3 medium tomatoes, chopped
1 stalk celery, chopped	1½ cups rice
	4 tablespoons grated parmesan cheese

LOMBARDY

Skin and bone chicken; dice flesh and set aside. Put veal, chicken bones and giblets into a pan with half the carrot, onion and celery. Cover with water, add a pinch of salt and cook stock over medium heat for about 30 minutes. Strain stock and keep hot. In a second pan, lightly brown remaining chopped vegetables in half the butter. Add diced chicken, season with salt and pepper and continue cooking, covered, for a few minutes. Pour in wine, reduce by half, add tomatoes and cook until soft. Pour in the rice and add a ladleful of the stock. Continue adding stock at intervals as rice dries out. When it is cooked, remove from heat, stir in remaining butter and half the parmesan. Allow to stand for a minute and then serve with remaining parmesan.   *Photograph page 119*

RISOTTO ALL'USO DI SARDEGNA
Sardinian risotto with tomato sauce

Ingredients/serves 4	1 clove garlic
5 tablespoons butter	½ stalk celery
1¾ cups rice	½ small onion
Salt and pepper	1 small bunch parsley
2 vegetable bouillon cubes	1lb tomatoes, chopped
For the sauce	Salt and pepper
⅓ cup chopped lean pancetta bacon	2 tablespoons grated pecorino cheese
Vegetable oil	

SARDINIA

Heat 3 tablespoons butter in a pan, add rice, season with salt and pepper and cook for a few minutes. Pour in 5 cups boiling water and crumble in bouillon cubes. Stir as rice absorbs water. Meanwhile, prepare sauce. Fry pancetta in a little oil, remove with a slotted spoon and set aside. Chop garlic, celery, onion and parsley together, add them to pancetta drippings and lightly brown. Add tomatoes, season with salt and pepper and cook for 15 minutes. Finally, add pancetta. Remove rice from heat, stir in remaining 2 tablespoons butter and cheese and pour hot sauce over.   *Photograph page 118*

SARDINIAN RISOTTO WITH TOMATO SAUCE
For recipe, see p.117

RISOTTO ALLA SBIRRAGLIA

CHICKEN RISOTTO
For recipe, see p.117

RISOTTO ALLA MILANESE
Milanese risotto

LOMBARDY

Ingredients/serves 4	1 cup dry white wine
2 tablespoons beef marrow	5 cups beef stock, skimmed of fat
1 small onion, thinly sliced	$\frac{1}{8}$ teaspoon saffron
$\frac{2}{3}$ cup butter	5 tablespoons grated parmesan
$1\frac{3}{4}$ cup rice	cheese

S crape marrow with a knife to remove any bits of bone, then chop and put in a pan with onion and $\frac{1}{3}$ cup butter. Fry until onion is soft but not brown. Add rice and fry for 2 or 3 minutes. Add wine and cook until absorbed. Add stock with a ladle, waiting between each addition until it has been absorbed. Cook rice for 30 minutes. Ten minutes before end of cooking time, dissolve saffron in a few tablespoons boiling stock and add to rice. Finally, add remaining $\frac{1}{3}$ cup butter and stir in parmesan. Let stand, covered, for 2 minutes before serving. *Photograph page 122*

RISOTTO ALLA PAESANA
Country-style risotto

LOMBARDY

Ingredients/serves 4	1 lb tomatoes, chopped
Vegetable oil	$\frac{1}{2}$ cup cooked white beans
1 onion, chopped	Salt and pepper
$\frac{1}{2}$ cup shelled fresh peas	$1\frac{3}{4}$ cups rice
$\frac{1}{2}$ cup asparagus tips	5 tablespoons butter
$\frac{3}{4}$ cup sliced zucchini	6 tablespoons grated parmesan
Chicken or beef stock	cheese

H eat a little oil in a pan, add onion and cook until soft. Add peas, asparagus and zucchini and cook for about 5 minutes. Add a little stock and cook over low heat for 10 minutes. Add tomatoes and beans; season with salt and pepper. Cook for 15 minutes, then add rice. Stir and add more stock, as necessary, and cook until al dente. Stir in the butter and 3 tablespoons parmesan. Serve sprinkled with remaining 3 tablespoons parmesan. *Photograph page 123*

RISOTTO ALLA TRASTEVERINA
Rice with ham and chicken livers

LAZIO, UMBRIA
AND
THE MARCHES

Ingredients/serves 4	½ cup sliced chicken livers
½ small onion, finely chopped	½ cup julienne-cut prosciutto
5 tablespoons, butter diced	1¾ cups rice
⅓ cup diced lean pancetta bacon	Chicken or beef stock
Salt and pepper	5 tablespoons grated parmesan cheese
½ cup dry marsala *or* red wine	

Fry onion in 2½ tablespoons butter, add pancetta, season with salt and pepper and cook gently for 2 minutes. Add marsala or red wine and let it evaporate almost completely. Stir in livers and prosciutto. Add rice and ladle on stock gradually as rice absorbs it, stirring constantly. Remove risotto from heat; stir in remaining 2½ tablespoons butter and a little parmesan. Leave to stand for 1 minute, then serve sprinkled with remaining 2½ tablespoons parmesan. *Photograph page 127*

RISO CON CARCIOFI ALLA SICILIANA
Sicilian artichoke risotto

SICILY

Ingredients/serves 4	½ cup peeled, seeded, minced tomato
5 tablespoons coarsley chopped bacon	Salt and pepper
1 onion	1¼ cups artichoke hearts packed in water, drained
1 clove garlic	
½ stalk celery	2½ cups cold water
1 bunch parsley	1 cup rice
Vegetable oil	¼ cup grated pecorino cheese

Chop together bacon, onion, garlic, celery and parsley and fry in a few tablespoons oil. Then add tomato crushed with a fork. Season with salt and pepper and cook gently for 10 minutes. Add artichoke hearts and cold water and cook for 10 minutes longer. Bring to a boil, add rice and cook for 20 minutes or until just tender. Stir in pecorino to serve.

RISOTTO ALLA MILANESE

Milanese risotto
For recipe, see p.120

RISOTTO ALLA PAESANA

COUNTRY-STYLE RISOTTO
For recipe, see p.120

RISOTTO CON LA ZUCCA
Pumpkin risotto

ABRUZZI-
MOLISE

Ingredients/serves 4	1 ¾ cups rice
1 lb pumpkin	2 chicken or beef bouillon cubes
½ cup butter	¼ cup grated parmesan cheese
4 cups boiling water	Salt

R emove seeds from pumpkin, then peel and cube. Place cubed pumpkin and ¼ cup butter in a saucepan and fry for a minute, add a ladleful of boiling water and cook gently until half cooked. Add rice to pumpkin, stir and fry for a minute; then add a ladleful of boiling water and crumble in bouillon cubes, stirring constantly and adding more water as each ladleful is absorbed. Continue process until rice is cooked. Turn off heat, add remaining ¼ cup butter and stir in parmesan. Season with salt to taste and serve.

RISOTTO CON LE TINCHE ALLA LOMBARDA
Tench risotto

LOMBARDY

Ingredients/serves 4	Salt and pepper
2 (½ lb) tench or 1 lb carp fillets	5 tablespoons butter
1 onion, cut into chunks	1 small bunch parsley, chopped
1 carrot, cut into chunks	1 clove garlic, chopped
1 stalk celery, cut into chunks	1 ¾ cups rice

C lean and scale tench, then wash thoroughly in running water. Blanch them for a few minutes to get rid of muddy taste. Then fillet them, reserving bones etc. Make a fish stock with fish trimmings, onion, carrot and celery. Season with salt and pepper, strain and keep warm. (If using carp fillets, substitute chicken stock for the fish stock.) Melt 3 tablespoons butter in a pan, add tench, season and cook gently. Keep warm. Melt remaining 2 tablespoons butter in a separate pan and add chopped parsley and garlic. When garlic has softened, add rice, stir for a few minutes and then gradually add fish stock, ladle by ladle, until rice is cooked. Stir to stop rice sticking. Put risotto into a deep dish, arrange fish fillets on top and serve. *Photograph page 126*

RISOTTO CON SCAMPI

Shrimp risotto

Ingredients/serves 4	$^2/_3$ cup dry white wine
6 tablespoons butter	1lb uncooked large shrimp,
Vegetable oil	shelled, deveined, cut into
$^1/_2$ carrot, chopped	chunks
$^1/_2$ small onion, chopped	6 cups chicken stock
1 stalk celery, chopped	$1^3/_4$ cups rice
About $^1/_4$ cup brandy	Salt
Pinch of dried leaf thyme	

VENETO

P reheat the oven to 400°F (205°C). Heat 3 tablespoons butter with 1 table-spoon oil in a pan, add chopped vegetables and cook until softened. Pour in brandy and add thyme. Cook gently, stirring, until liquid has evaporated. Then add wine and reduce by half. Add shrimp and cook for 15 minutes. Keep hot. Bring stock to a boil, pour in rice and add a pinch of salt. Bring back to boil, then cover and bake for 20 minutes. Drain rice, fluff with a fork, mix in the remaining 3 tablespoons butter and pour shrimp mixture over it.

RISOTTO CON LE COZZE ALLA GONDOLIERA

Mussel risotto

Ingredients/serves 4	6 tablespoons butter
2 lbs mussels	$1^3/_4$ cups rice
Vegetable oil	Salt and pepper
3 cloves garlic, chopped	Fish stock or salted water
$^1/_2$ small onion, chopped	

VENETO

P ull off and discard beards from mussels; wash mussels thoroughly in running water. Put them into a big pan with a little oil and half the garlic and put over a gentle heat. As mussels open, remove them from their shells and set aside. Strain cooking liquid and reserve. Soften remaining garlic and the onion in 4 tablespoons butter and a little oil. Add rice. Season with salt and freshly ground pepper, adding fish stock or salted water a ladleful at a time until rice is tender. Just before removing from heat, stir in mussels and strained mussel liquid; add remaining 2 tablespoons butter and serve. *Photograph page 130*

RISOTTO CON LE TINCHE ALLA LOMBARDA

TENCH RISOTTO
For recipe, see p.124

RISOTTO ALLA TRASTEVERINA

*R*ICE WITH HAM AND CHICKEN LIVERS
For recipe, see p.121

RISOTTO ALLA PARMIGIANA
Parmesan risotto

EMILIA-
ROMAGNA

Ingredients/serves 4	1¾ cups rice
1 small onion	6 tablespoons grated parmesan
⅔ cup butter	cheese
Olive oil	Salt
5 cups beef stock, skimmed of fat	

T hinly slice the onion and put in a pan with 4 tablespoons butter and 1 tablespoon oil; cook over low heat until soft but not brown, adding 1 tablespoon stock, if necessary. Add the rice and fry for a minute, then add a ladleful of stock. When this has been absorbed, add another and repeat process until 2½ cups stock have been used. Stir in half the remaining butter and 2 tablespoons parmesan. Continue adding stock gradually. When rice is cooked, season with salt, add remaining butter and parmesan and serve.

RISO CON ASPARAGI ALLA SICILIANA
Rice with asparagus

SICILY

Ingredients/serves 4	1 clove garlic, chopped
1 lb asparagus	1 bunch parsley, chopped
Vegetable oil	Salt
6 tablespoons chopped bacon	1¼ cups rice
1 onion, chopped	½ cup diced caciocavallo cheese

C lean asparagus, cut off tough stalk ends and boil for 12 minutes in salted water. Drain, reserving cooking liquid; cut off asparagus tips. (Reserve remaining asparagus for other uses.) In a pan, heat oil and fry the bacon, onion, garlic and parsley. Pour on a little asparagus liquid, season with salt and bring to the boil. Add rice, adding more asparagus liquid as it is absorbed. When rice is cooked, mix in cheese and asparagus tips.   *Photograph page 131*

RISO CON LE FAVE ALLA SICILIANA

Rice with lima beans

Ingredients/serves 4	2 medium tomatoes, peeled,
3 strips bacon	chopped, crushed with a fork
I onion	Salt and pepper
I clove garlic	I ½ cups shelled fresh lima
½ stalk celery	I ¾ cups rice
I bunch parsley	Grated pecorino cheese
Vegetable oil	

SICILY

Chop bacon, onion, garlic, celery and parsley finely together. Heat a little oil in a pan and cook mixture gently, stirring. Add tomatoes, season with salt and pepper and cook for 10 minutes. Add lima beans and 6 cups water. Bring to a boil and add rice. Cook for 20 minutes or until rice is done and the consistency is thick and soupy. Sprinkle with pecorino to serve.

RISI E BISI

Rice and peas

Ingredients/serves 4	Olive oil
2 ¾ lbs unshelled fresh peas	6 cups beef stock
I onion	I ¼ cups rice
2-3 strips lean pancetta bacon	5 tablespoons grated parmesan
2 tablespoons chopped parsley	cheese
6 tablespoons butter	Salt and pepper

VENETO

This Venetian rice dish should be more like a thick soup than a dry risotto. Shell peas and put into cold water. Chop onion and bacon, put in a pan with parsley, 3 tablespoons butter and 2 tablespoons oil, and cook until onion has softened. Add drained peas and a ladleful of stock, stir and cook for 10 minutes. When peas are half cooked, add remaining stock. Bring it back to a boil, add rice and cook gently, stirring to prevent it from sticking to the bottom. Remove from heat, add remaining 3 tablespoons butter, stir in parmesan, season with salt and pepper and serve.

RISOTTO CON LE COZZE ALLA GONDOLIERA

MUSSEL RISOTTO
For recipe, see p.125

RISO CON ASPARAGI ALLA SICILIANA

RICE WITH ASPARAGUS
For recipe, see p.128

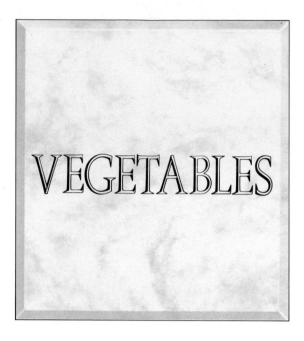

VEGETABLES

Fresh vegetables are the delight of the Italian market place. Fennel, baby peas, artichokes, asparagus, lima beans, chestnuts, funghi, eggplant, peppers, zucchini and tomatoes are all eaten in their proper seasons, and often make a complete course in themselves.

RADICCHIO ROSSO DI TREVISO IN PADELLA
Fried radicchio

Ingredients/serves 4	Virgin olive oil
8 heads radicchio	Salt and pepper

VENETO

W ash radicchio well without removing leaves and drain off as much water as possible. Then cut into quarters from stem to tip and squeeze out more excess water (otherwise oil will spit when heated). Put them on a plate and sprinkle with oil, salt and freshly ground pepper. Put a large skillet on to heat and, when hot, put in radicchio and cook briskly, turning over as soon as each side is cooked. Arrange on a serving dish. This method results in crisp radicchio — for softer radicchio, cook, covered, over lower heat.

CAVOLO CON PANCETTA E PATATE
Cabbage with bacon and potatoes

Ingredients/serves 6	Chicken stock
1 (about 2 lb) head savoy cabbage	Salt and pepper
	Ground nutmeg
About ¾ cup butter	1¼ lbs potatoes
¾ cup chopped smoked pancetta bacon	Milk
	2 egg yolks

ABRUZZI-MOLISE

P reheat oven to 350°F (175°C). Trim cabbage and blanch in salted water for 10 minutes. Drain and squeeze out water, then chop coarsely. Heat a little butter in a large pan, add pancetta and cabbage, stir well and cover with stock. Season with salt, pepper and nutmeg and bring to a boil, then simmer over medium heat for 45 minutes. Boil potatoes in another pan. Peel, then press through a strainer or mash well while still hot. Put mashed potatoes in a small saucepan over medium heat, add 4 tablespoons butter and enough milk to give a soft, but not runny, consistency. Season and mix in egg yolks. Butter baking dish, spoon in cabbage mixture and pipe on mashed potatoes. Dot top with remaining butter and bake for 10 minutes. Serve hot. *Photograph page 134*

SAVOY CABBAGE STUFFED WITH SCAMORZA CHEESE
For recipe, see p.136

CABBAGE WITH BACON AND POTATOES
For recipe, see p.133

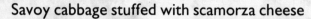
VERZA RIPIENA CON SCAMORZA ALLA NAPOLETANA

Savoy cabbage stuffed with scamorza cheese

CAMPANIA

Ingredients/serves 4	1¼ lbs tomatoes, peeled,
1 (1lb) head savoy cabbage	seeded, pressed through a
1½ cups thinly sliced scamorza	strainer
or mozzarella cheese	Salt and pepper
Vegetable oil	Few tablespoons grated
1 tablespoon chopped onion	parmesan cheese

P reheat the oven to 350°F (175°C). Trim cabbage stem and remove outer leaves. Boil or steam whole cabbage until cooked but still firm. Allow to cool. Remove leaves and divide into 8 piles. Fill top leaf in each pile with scamorza or mozzarella and roll up each pile around cheese. Heat a little oil in a skillet and fry onion until soft. Add tomatoes, season with salt and pepper and cook over medium heat until very soft, being careful not to let it dry out. Put a layer of tomato sauce in a baking dish, arrange cabbage rolls on top and pour remaining sauce over. Sprinkle with parmesan, bake for 10 minutes and serve hot. *Photograph page 134*

FAVE FRESCHE AL GUANCIALE

Lima beans with bacon

TUSCANY

Ingredients/serves 4	1 small onion, sliced
4½ lbs unshelled fresh lima	1 cup chicken stock
beans	Salt and pepper
⅔ cup diced pancetta, *or* bacon	
1½ tablespoons solid vegetable	
shortening *or* butter	

S hell beans and put in a bowl of cold water. You should have about 2 pounds shelled beans. Put pancetta or bacon in a large pan, add shortening or butter and fry gently to render bacon fat. Then add well-drained beans and onion. Pour in stock, season lightly, cover and cook briskly for about 40 minutes, stirring frequently. Transfer to a deep, preheated serving dish. You could serve this garnished with triangles of toast.

CIPOLLINE NOVELLE ALLA ESCOFFIER
New onions Escoffier

Ingredients/serves 4	
1¾ lbs small white onions	1 teaspoon fennel seeds
Vegetable oil	3 tablespoons golden raisins, soaked in lukewarm water until
Salt and pepper	plump
1 bay leaf	½ cup dry white wine
Pinch of dried leaf thyme	About ¼ cup Cognac

VENETO

Peel onions and boil for 5 minutes. Drain and pat dry. Heat some oil in a pan, add onions, season with salt and pepper and fry gently until golden brown, being careful not to let them burn. Add bay leaf, thyme, fennel seeds and golden raisins, and pour in wine and cognac. Bring to a boil, cover and cook for 5 minutes longer. Remove from the heat, allow to cool and serve.

Photograph page 139

ZUCCHINI ALLA PAESANA
Country-style zucchini

Ingredients/serves 4	
1 lb zucchini	1 lb tomatoes, peeled, seeded, chopped
1 egg	1½ teaspoons sugar
Salt	Pepper
⅓ cup breadcrumbs	½ cup grated parmesan cheese
Butter	1 tablespoon chopped fresh basil
Vegetable oil	4 fresh mint leaves, chopped
1 onion, sliced	

ABRUZZI-MOLISE

Preheat oven to 350°F (175°C). Cut ends off zucchini and cut lengthwise. Beat egg with a little salt. Dip zucchini in egg, and then in breadcrumbs. Melt a little butter in a pan with some oil and fry zucchini until golden. Drain on paper towels. Set aside. Heat ¼ cup oil in a pan and cook the onion for 5 minutes. Add tomatoes, sugar, salt and pepper, cover and cook over medium heat for 30 minutes, stirring occasionally. Butter a baking dish, put in a layer of zucchini, cover with a little tomato sauce, sprinkle with parmesan, basil and mint, and continue the layers like this until all ingredients have been used up. End with sauce and bake for 15 minutes. This dish can be served hot but is also delicious lukewarm or cold.

AUBERGINES WITH TOMATOES
For recipe, see p.144

NEW ONIONS ESCOFFIER
For recipe, see p.137

FONDI DI CARCIOFI ALLA FIORENTINA
Artichoke hearts with spinach

TUSCANY

Ingredients/serves 4	For the sauce
8 artichoke hearts	¼ cup butter
Juice of 1 lemon	2 tablespoons all-purpose flour
Olive oil	⅔ cup milk
All-purpose flour	⅔ cup whipping cream
1¼ lbs fresh spinach	Salt and pepper
3 tablespoons butter	Ground nutmeg
Salt and pepper	¼ cup shredded swiss cheese
1 tablespoon grated parmesan cheese	To assemble
	2 tablespoons grated parmesan cheese
	3 tablespoons breadcrumbs
	1 tablespoon butter

Preheat oven to 375°F (190°C). Steam or boil artichoke hearts in water acidulated with lemon juice, to which you have added 1 tablespoon oil and 1 teaspoon flour. Meanwhile trim and wash spinach in several changes of water, then boil in water clinging to the leaves. When cooked, rinse in cold water and squeeze dry. Melt 3 tablespoons butter in a pan, add spinach, season with salt and pepper and cook over low heat until butter is absorbed. Then stir in 1 tablespoon parmesan. *For the sauce,* melt ¼ cup butter in a small pan and add the flour, blending well with a wooden spoon to avoid lumps forming. Add milk and cream, season with salt, pepper and nutmeg and cook, stirring, until sauce has thickened and is simmering. Stir in cheese and remove from heat. *To assemble,* grease a large baking dish. Cut a thin slice off bottom of artichoke hearts so that they stand upright and arrange them in dish. Divide spinach between them, mounding equally on top, pour over the sauce, sprinkle with 2 tablespoons parmesan and breadcrumbs and dot with 1 tablespoon butter. Bake for about 10 minutes or until golden on top. Serve at once.

ASPARAGI ALLA MILANESE
Asparagus with eggs and cheese

Ingredients/serves 4	6 tablespoons butter
3 lbs asparagus	3 tablespoons grated parmesan
4 eggs	cheese

LOMBARDY

Clean asparagus and cut off tough stalk ends; boil or steam asparagus. Drain and arrange on a heated serving dish. Fry eggs in about 4 tablespoons butter just until set. Heat remaining butter separately. Sprinkle parmesan on asparagus, put just-set eggs carefully on top, then drizzle with melted butter. Serve at once.

POLPETTONE DI BIETOLE ALLA LIGURE
Beets with cream and mushrooms

Ingredients/serves 4	2 eggs
5 tablespoons butter	3 tablespoons whipping cream
Vegetable oil	1 1/2 tablespoons grated
1 1/2 cups sliced fresh	parmesan cheese
mushrooms	Salt and pepper
1 clove garlic, chopped	Breadcrumbs
3 lbs beets, cooked, peeled,	
chopped	

LIGURIA

Preheat oven to 350°F (175°C). Melt butter with a little oil in a skillet, add mushrooms and garlic and fry until soft. Stir in beets and cook gently so that flavors mingle. Put eggs in a bowl with cream and parmesan and beat together well. Season with salt and pepper. Add beet mixture and stir well to coat in egg mixture. Grease a baking dish, sprinkle with breadcrumbs and fill with beet mixture, levelling off top. Sprinkle with breadcrumbs again, drizzle a little oil over top and bake until golden.

SPINACI ALLA ROMANO

SPINACH ROMAN STYLE
For recipe, see p.145

RUSTICANA ALLA PIACENTINA

COUNTRY-STYLE PEPPERS AND TOMATOES
For recipe, see p.145

PORRI CON BESCIAMELLA

Leeks in béchamel sauce

EMILIA-
ROMAGNA

Ingredients/serves 4	1 cup béchamel sauce with 1
1 ¼ lbs leeks	egg yolk added
2 tablespoons butter	¼ cup grated gruyère cheese
⅓ cup julienne-cut cooked ham	

Preheat oven to 400°F (205°C). Trim leeks, discarding green tops, and wash well. Boil in lightly salted water, drain and arrange in a baking dish. Dot with butter, cover with ham and pour béchamel sauce over top. Sprinkle with gruyère and bake until golden brown.

MELANZANE AL POMODORI

Eggplants with tomatoes

CALABRIA

Ingredients/serves 4	Salt and pepper
4 large eggplants	1 ¼ cups seeded, chopped
Vegetable oil	tomatoes
2 cloves garlic, crushed	

Cut off ends of eggplants. Wash eggplants (do not peel); then cut them into chunks. Heat some oil in a pan and fry garlic until soft. Add eggplants and season with salt and pepper. Cook gently for 10 minutes. Add tomatoes and continue to cook over low heat for 20 minutes or until eggplants are done. Pile into a dish and serve. *Photograph page 139*

SPINACI ALLA ROMANA
Spinach Roman style

Ingredients/serves 4	3 tablespoons golden raisins,
2 lbs fresh spinach	soaked in lukewarm water until
Vegetable oil	plump
1 clove garlic, crushed	Salt
1/3 cup finely diced bacon	Butter
3 tablespoons pine nuts	

LAZIO, UMBRIA AND THE MARCHES

Wash spinach, discarding tough stalks and discolored leaves. Cook gently in water clinging to leaves, then drain and squeeze dry. Heat a little oil in a pan, add garlic, bacon and spinach, and cook, gently stirring. After a few minutes, add pine nuts and golden raisins. Remove from heat, season with salt, put in a serving dish, top with about 1 tablespoon butter and serve.

Photograph page 142

RUSTICANA ALLA PIACENTINA
Country-style peppers and tomatoes

Ingredients/serves 4	1 lb tomatoes, peeled, seeded,
1/4 cup butter	chopped
Vegetable oil	Salt
1 lb green onions	4 hard-cooked eggs, chopped
4 large green or yellow bell	
peppers, seeded, cut into strips	

EMILIA-ROMAGNA

Heat butter with some oil in a pan and fry the green onions and peppers until half cooked. (If desired, you may roast and peel peppers before sautéing with onions.) Then add tomatoes, season with salt, add a little lukewarm water and cook over medium heat, stirring occasionally. As soon as peppers are cooked, stir in eggs and serve. *Photograph page 143*

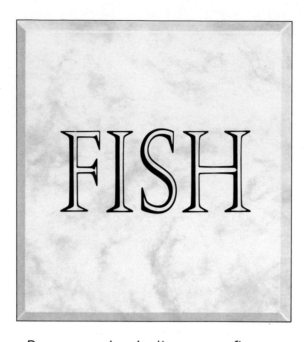

FISH

Because the Italians are firm believers in using only fresh local produce, you will be unlikely to find seafood in Italy at any distance from the coast. Fish — whether from sea or rivers — is perhaps at its best simply cooked with butter or olive oil, a few leaves of sage and served with a wedge of lemon.

TROTA SALMONATA CON AGLIATA ALLA LIGURE
Salmon trout with aïoli

LIGURIA

Ingredients/serves 4	
1 (2-lb) salmon trout (or use a large trout)	4 cloves garlic
	2 slices white bread, crusts trimmed, softened in vinegar
2 small carrots, chopped	Salt and pepper
1 stalk celery, chopped	1 cup vegetable oil
2 small onions, chopped	Lemon wedges
1 tablespoon chopped parsley	$\frac{1}{4}$ cup butter, melted
3 medium potatoes, peeled, sliced	

C lean and wash trout, put in a fish kettle or a pan that it will fit and cover with a court bouillon made from 6 cups water, the carrots, celery, onions and parsley. Bring to a gentle boil and simmer for 12 minutes or until fish is done. Boil potatoes in salted water. In a mortàr, pound garlic with the bread, season with salt and pepper and gradually add oil, as if you were making mayonnaise. Drain trout, put onto a dish and surround with lemon wedges. Drain potatoes, drizzle with melted butter, and serve with fish; pass aïoli separately.

Photograph page 148

RAZZA CON BURRO DI ACCIUGHE
Skate with anchovy butter

CAMPANIA

Ingredients/serves 4	
2 lbs skate	Salt and pepper
2 small carrots, chopped	1 tablespoon capers
1 stalk celery, chopped	1 tablespoon sliced dill pickle
2 small onions, chopped	1 tablespoon chopped parsley
5 tablespoons butter	Squeeze of lemon juice
$\frac{1}{4}$ cup all-purpose flour	5 flat anchovy fillets soaked in milk

P oach skate in a court bouillon made from 3 cups water, the carrots, celery and onions. When fish is cooked, transfer to a serving platter and keep warm. Melt $2\frac{1}{2}$ tablespoons butter, blend in flour and a little fish poaching liquid. Season with salt and pepper and simmer, stirring, for 7-8 minutes until sauce has thickened and is smooth and velvety. Add capers, dill pickle, parsley and lemon juice. Drain anchovies and pound with remaining $2\frac{1}{2}$ tablespoons butter. Blend anchovy butter into sauce. Heat through, pour over skate and serve.

Photograph page 148

SALMON TROUT WITH AÏOLI
For recipe, see p.147

RAZZA CON BURRO DI ACCIUGHE

SKATE WITH ANCHOVY BUTTER
For recipe, see p.147

Sarde Fritte alla Ligure
Fried stuffed sardines

LIGURIA

Ingredients/serves 4	1 clove garlic, crushed
16 fresh sardines	1 teaspoon chopped fresh
Olive oil	marjoram
2 tablespoons dried	Pinch of dried leaf oregano
mushrooms, soaked, drained	4 eggs
1 tablespoon fresh	Salt and pepper
breadcrumbs, softened in a	All-purpose flour
little milk and squeezed dry	Fine dry breadcrumbs
1 tablespoon grated	
parmesan cheese	

Clean sardines, removing heads and tails. Open them out, remove bones, wash and pat dry. Heat a little olive oil in a skillet, chop mushrooms finely and fry gently for a few minutes. Transfer them to a dish and add fresh breadcrumbs, parmesan, garlic, marjoram, oregano, 2 eggs and a pinch of salt. Stuff sardines with this mixture, then close them up. Beat remaining 2 eggs with salt and pepper. Dip stuffed sardines first into flour, then into seasoned beaten egg, then into dry breadcrumbs. Fry in hot oil and serve immediately.

Photograph page 152

Sarde a Beccaficu Catanese
Baked stuffed sardines

CALABRIA

Ingredients/serves 4	All-purpose flour
16 fresh sardines	2 eggs, beaten
2 tablespoons vinegar	Breadcrumbs
Salt and pepper	Olive oil
⅔ cup mixed chopped garlic,	Lemon wedges
chopped parsley and grated	
parmesan cheese	

Preheat oven to 375°F (190°C). Clean sardines, removing heads and tails, open them out and remove bones. Wash and pat dry. Arrange on a big dish, sprinkle with vinegar, salt and pepper and stuff each one with garlic, parsley and cheese mixture. Close fish up again, pressing down well; dip them first in flour, then in beaten egg and then in breadcrumbs. Put sardines in a greased baking dish, sprinkle with oil and bake for 25-30 minutes. Serve with lemon wedges.

SGOMBRI ALLA CALABRESE
Mackerel with anchovy butter

Ingredients/serves 4	2 tablespoons anchovy paste
2 (1-lb) mackerel	2 tablespoons butter
Olive oil	1 teaspoon parsley
Salt and pepper	Lemon juice

CALABRIA

C lean mackerel, remove heads, open them out and remove backbones. Wash and pat dry. Sprinkle with oil, broil or barbecue over wood, and season well with salt and pepper. For anchovy butter, mix anchovy paste, butter, parsley and lemon juice to taste. Pass anchovy butter separately.

STOCCAFISSO ALLA SICILIANA
Dried cod Sicilian style

Ingredients/serves 4	Salt and pepper
1¾ lbs dried cod, already soaked	¾ cup pitted ripe olives
	1½ tablespoons capers
Olive oil	1 tablespoon golden raisins,
1 small onion, chopped	soaked in lukewarm water until
1 large clove garlic, chopped	plump
½ cup white wine	1 tablespoon pine nuts
1¼ lbs tomatoes, peeled, seeded, pressed through a strainer	3 medium potatoes, peeled, sliced

SICILY

P reheat oven to 375°F (190°C). Remove bones and skin from cod and cut flesh into cubes. Heat some oil in an ovenproof saucepan, fry onion and garlic and add fish. Cook for a minute, then add wine. When wine has almost evaporated, add tomatoes and enough water to cover fish. Season with salt and freshly ground pepper. Bring to a boil, cover and bake for an hour. Add olives, capers, golden raisins, pine nuts and potatoes. Continue to bake until potatoes are done and serve immediately. *Photograph page 152*

*F*RIED *STUFFED SARDINES*
For recipe, see p.150

STOCCAFISSO ALLA SICILIANA

*D*RIED *COD SICILIAN STYLE*
For recipe, see p.151

TOTANI O CALAMARI IN ZIMINO ALLA GENOVESE

Squid or calamari in a spicy sauce

LIGURIA

Ingredients/serves 4	
1 ¼ lbs small squid	Olive oil
2 tablespoons chopped parsley	½ cup dry white wine
2 cloves garlic	1 tablespoon tomato paste
1 onion	Salt and pepper
1 stalk celery	2 lbs beets

C lean squid and cut into strips, then wash and drain. Chop together parsley, one clove of garlic, onion and celery. Put into a large skillet with some oil and fry over medium heat for a few minutes. Add squid and continue to fry, gradually adding the white wine. When it has evaporated add tomato paste, dissolved in ½ cup water. Season with salt and pepper and cook gently, stirring occasionally. Meanwhile, trim beets, wash well and cut into small pieces. Heat ¼ cup oil in a pan and add the second clove of garlic, crushed. Cook until garlic begins to brown. Then add beets, season well, stir, cover pan and cook gently for 10 minutes. Remove garlic; add beets to squid and cook 10 minutes longer. Serve on a platter with triangles of toast.

SOGLIOLE ALL'ERBA SALVIA
Sole with sage

Ingredients/serves 4	All-purpose flour
2 eggs, beaten	Breadcrumbs
Salt and pepper	Vegetable oil
8 sole fillets	Few fresh sage leaves

VENETO

S eason beaten eggs with salt and pepper. Dip sole fillets in flour, then in seasoned beaten egg, then in breadcrumbs, pressing them well on with your fingers. Fry fish and sage leaves in plenty of hot oil until fish is golden brown; drain on paper towels and sprinkle with salt. Arrange on a serving dish and serve with boiled potatoes. *Photograph page 156*

SCAMPI GRIGLIATA
Broiled jumbo shrimp

Ingredients/serves 4	Salt and pepper
2 lbs jumbo shrimp	½ cup butter
Olive oil	2 cloves garlic, crushed

VENETO

W ash shrimp and pat dry. Lay them in a dish and pour over enough olive oil to coat. Season well with salt and pepper, cover and let marinate for an hour, stirring occasionally. Melt the butter with the crushed garlic in a small saucepan over low heat, stirring. Remove from the heat and set aside. Meanwhile, thread shrimp onto wooden skewers. Brush with oil from marinade and broil for 15-20 minutes, turning once. They should be nicely browned. Remove shrimp from skewers and arrange them on a serving dish. Pass garlic butter separately. *Photograph page 156*

SOGLIOLE ALL'ERBA SALVIA

SOLE WITH SAGE
For recipe, see p.155

SCAMPI GRIGLIATA

BROILED JUMBO SHRIMP
For recipe, see p.155

TRIGLIE AL PROSCIUTTO
Red mullet with ham

LAZIO, UMBRIA
AND
THE MARCHES

Ingredients/serves 4	Olive oil
12 small red mullet	1/4 cup breadcrumbs
Salt	Pepper
12 slices prosciutto	1 tablespoon chopped parsley
4 ripe tomatoes	Juice of 1/2 lemon
1 clove garlic	

Clean and scale fish; wash, pat dry and season with salt. Wrap each one in a slice of prosciutto. Peel tomatoes, then seed and slice. Cook garlic for 5 minutes in a pan with some oil. Add mullet and cook for 2-3 minutes on each side, turning them gently. Add tomatoes, sprinkle with breadcrumbs, season with salt and pepper and cook over low heat for 10 minutes. Sprinkle with parsley and lemon juice. Put mullet on a dish and serve. *Photograph page 161*

TRIGLIE ALLA LIVORNESE
Red mullet Livorno style

TUSCANY

Ingredients/serves 4	4 red mullet *or* 4 (1/2-lb) redfish
1 lb ripe tomatoes	1 stalk celery
2 tablespoons butter	1 clove garlic
Olive oil	1/4 cup chopped parsley
Few fresh basil leaves, chopped	All-purpose flour
Salt and pepper	

Wash tomatoes, peel and press through a strainer. In a small pan, heat the butter, 2 tablespoons oil and the basil, then add the tomatoes, season with salt and pepper and cook gently for 30 minutes. Meanwhile, clean and scale fish and remove the fins; wash fish and pat dry. Finely chop celery and garlic. Place celery, garlic, parsley and about 1/4 cup oil into a pan which you can bring to the table. Fry for a few minutes. Lightly flour the fish and brown on one side. Remove from the heat and very carefully (mullet are fragile) turn them over. Put them back on the heat. Pour over the tomato sauce and cook for about 10 minutes. Serve fish in the pan. *Photograph page 160*

POLPI AFFOGATI ALLA LUCIANA

Octopus in tomato sauce

Ingredients/serves 4	2 medium tomatoes, peeled,
2 (1-lb) rock octopuses	chopped
Salt	1 red chili pepper
2 tablespoons chopped parsley	About ¼ cup vegetable oil
	Lemon wedges

APULIA

C lean the octopuses, then peel off the skin and pound them to tenderize. Wash octopuses and place in a heatproof ceramic dish. Season with salt and add the parsley, tomatoes, chili pepper and oil. Cover the dish tightly with 2 sheets of waxed paper, and secure with the lid or with string. Cook over very low heat for about 2 hours. Remove the chili pepper, cut the octopuses into pieces and serve in the cooking dish. Accompany with lemon wedges.

SEPPIE AI PISELLI

Squid with peas

Ingredients/serves 4	1½ lbs unshelled fresh peas
Handful of fresh basil leaves	¼ cup butter
1 large bunch parsley	½ cup dry white wine
1 stalk celery	3 cups peeled, seeded, chopped
1 clove garlic	ripe tomatoes
1 onion	1 bay leaf
2 lbs squid	Salt and pepper

VENETO

C hop together the basil, parsley, celery, garlic and onion. Clean the squid. Remove the eyes. Wash thoroughly and peel away the outer membranes. Remove the transparent pen. Slice the body and the tentacles. Shell peas and place in a saucepan of cold water. Put the butter in a heavy saucepan and set over heat to melt. Add the chopped vegetables and cook until soft. Stir in the squid and pour over the white wine. Cook for a few minutes or until the wine has almost evaporated. Stir in the tomatoes and drained peas. Add the bay leaf and season with salt and pepper. Cover and cook over medium heat for about 1 hour, stirring occasionally to ensure that sauce does not stick to bottom of pan. Serve hot with rice, potatoes or polenta.

TRIGLIE ALLA LIVORNESE

RED MULLET LIVORNO STYLE
For recipe, see p.158

TRIGLIE AL PROSCIUTTO

*R*ED MULLET WITH HAM
For recipe, se p.158

POULTRY
AND
GAME

Poultry and game, for Italians who live in the country or in the poorer south, are virtually free foods. Many families have chickens scratching about in their back yards and hunting is a national pastime, be it for pheasant, quail, rabbit, hare or even wild boar.

POLLO RIPIENO AI CARCIOFI
Chicken stuffed with artichokes

Ingredients/serves 4	4 cooked artichoke hearts
1 clove garlic	1 lemon, pierced in several
Rosemary sprig	places
2 tablespoons butter	4 fresh sage leaves
Salt and pepper	2 tablespoons olive oil
1 (about 3-lb) broiler-fryer	About $\frac{3}{4}$ cup dry white wine

EMILIA-
ROMAGNA

Preheat oven to 350°F (175°C). Crush garlic and rosemary. Put in a bowl with butter, salt and pepper; mix with a wooden spoon until finely creamed. Wash chicken, pat dry and stuff with artichokes and lemon. Sew up opening with cooking thread. Skewer chicken together with a thin skewer, putting 1 sage leaf under each wing and each leg. Rub butter mixture all over chicken, then sprinkle with salt and pepper. Put in a baking pan or dish and pour oil over. Roast for $1\frac{1}{2}$ hours, turning frequently. Remove from oven when golden brown. Transfer to a serving plate and cut into pieces. Arrange artichoke hearts around chicken. Discard lemon. Pour wine into pan and heat over low heat, stirring to blend wine and dripping. Pour sauce over chicken and serve at once.

Photograph page 165

POLLO CON PEPERONATA
Chicken with peppers

Ingredients/serves 4	5 small bell peppers, seeded,
$\frac{1}{4}$ cup vegetable oil	cut into strips
2 tablespoons butter	1 onion, sliced
2 lbs chicken pieces	Salt and pepper
$\frac{1}{2}$ cup dry white wine	Chicken stock
1 lb ripe tomatoes, peeled,	2 tablespoons chopped fresh
halved	basil

APULIA

Heat oil and butter together in a pan, add chicken pieces and brown for 5 minutes. Pour over wine and reduce. Add tomatoes, bell peppers and onion; season with salt and pepper, then add about 1 cup stock and cook over low heat for $1\frac{1}{2}$ hours. Add more stock as needed. Sprinkle with basil and serve.

Photograph page 165

CHICKEN STUFFED WITH ARTICHOKES
For recipe, see p.163

POLLO CON PEPERONATA

CHICKEN WITH PEPPERS
For recipe, see p.163

FILETTI DI TACCHINO ALLA BOLOGNESE
Turkey breast Bologna style

EMILIA-
ROMAGNA

Ingredients/serves 4	Salt and pepper
1 ¼ lbs turkey breast, sliced	About 1 cup beef stock
½ cup butter	1 white truffle (optional)
All-purpose flour	¼ cup grated parmesan cheese
Dry marsala	

Pound turkey slices flat. Choose a pan large enough to accommodate them in one layer. Heat ¼ cup butter in pan until it browns. Flour turkey slices and fry quickly on both sides. Sprinkle on a few tablespoons marsala, season with salt and pepper and cook until wine has evaporated. Remove turkey with a slotted spoon. Pour half the stock into pan. Bring to boil and add turkey slices, turning to let them absorb flavor. Cook over low heat for a few minutes. If using truffle, wash it in a little white wine, then cut into thin slices. Preheat oven to 375°F (190°C). Put turkey in a greased baking dish. Add a little stock to sauce left in pan and cook over high heat, stirring well to dissolve any sediment left at bottom. Cover turkey with truffle slices (if used), sprinkle with parmesan, top evenly with sauce from pan, and dot with remaining ¼ cup butter. Cover and put in oven until cheese melts. Serve with creamed potatoes, asparagus tips, buttered spinach or glazed onions.

ANITRA ALL'ACCIUGA
Duck with anchovies

ABRUZZI-
MOLISE

Ingredients/serves 4	Few slices fresh gingerroot
10 flat anchovy fillets	½ cup pitted green olives
8 cloves garlic, chopped	Vegetable oil
1 onion, sliced	1 (about 4-lb) duck, cut up
1 carrot, sliced	Salt
1 stalk celery, sliced	Chicken stock

Put anchovies, garlic, vegetables, ginger and olives into a large saucepan. Coat with a few tablespoons oil and fry for 5 minutes. Add duck pieces to pan with very little salt (anchovies are salty) and brown over high heat. Cover and cook over medium heat for 45 minutes, adding a little stock as necessary to prevent duck from drying out. *Photograph page 168*

FAGIANO ARROSTO CON UVA E NOCI
Roast pheasant with grapes and walnuts

LAZIO, UMBRIA
AND
THE MARCHES

Ingredients/serves 4	12 walnuts, shelled
1 pheasant	2 tablespoons brandy
4 strips pancetta bacon	Salt and pepper
2 lbs green grapes	2 tablespoons butter
About ½ pint dairy sour cream (1 cup)	

Wrap pheasant in pancetta and secure with a thin skewer. Set aside a quarter of the grapes and press the rest through a strainer or purée in a blender. Drain off juice and reserve. Put pheasant in a pan; add sour cream, walnuts, brandy, grape juice and a pinch of salt and pepper. Cover and cook over low heat for an hour, stirring frequently. Preheat oven to 475°F (245°C). Remove pheasant from pan and take off pancetta slices. Line a roasting pan with foil and put the pheasant in it. Roast for 10 minutes or until golden brown. Meanwhile, remove walnuts from pheasant simmering liquid and set aside. Boil liquid over high heat until reduced to ½ cup. Add butter and stir until it melts. Put pheasant on a serving dish and surround with walnuts and reserved grapes. Pour boiling sauce over the pheasant and serve at once.

CONIGLIO CON PEPERONI
Rabbit with peppers

APULIA

Ingredients/serves 4	Salt and pepper
1 rabbit, cut up	Chicken stock
¼ cup butter	4 bell peppers, seeded, sliced
¼ cup vegetable oil	4 flat anchovy fillets, chopped
Rosemary sprig	2 cloves garlic, crushed
1 bay leaf	2 tablespoons vinegar

Brown rabbit pieces in a pan with 2 tablespoons butter, 2 tablespoons oil, the rosemary and bay leaf. Season with salt and pepper; cook over low heat for 1½ hours, adding stock as necessary to keep meat moist. In another saucepan heat remaining 2 tablespoons butter and 2 tablespoons oil; add bell peppers, anchovies, garlic and vinegar. Season and cook gently for 20 minutes. Add pepper sauce to rabbit, let flavors mingle for 5 minutes and then serve. *Photograph page 169*

ANITRA ALL'ACCIUGA

DUCK WITH ANCHOVIES
For recipe, see p.166

CONIGLIO CON PEPERONI

RABBIT WITH PEPPERS
For recipe, see p.167

QUAGLIE CON PANCETTA
Quail with pancetta bacon

LAZIO, UMBRIA AND THE MARCHES

Ingredients/serves 4	3 medium potatoes
8 (4-6-oz) quail	4 strips lean smoked pancetta
Salt and pepper	bacon, blanched
8 thin strips bacon	Chicken stock
½ cup butter	

Wash quail, pat dry, sprinkle with salt and pepper and truss each with a skewer. Wrap thin bacon strips around quail, securing with thread. Melt ¼ cup butter in a pan, put in quail and cook, turning occasionally. Peel potatoes, cut into strips and fry until browned in remaining ¼ cup butter with a pinch of salt. Drain quail, reserving juices; remove skewers, arrange on a dish and garnish with fried potatoes and pancetta. Add a few tablespoons stock to cooking juices from quail, using a wooden spoon to scrape off browned particles sticking to bottom of pan. Heat through, stirring; pour sauce onto quail and serve.

QUAGLIE AL BRANDY ALLA ROMANA
Quail in brandy with peas

LAZIO, UMBRIA AND THE MARCHES

Ingredients/serves 4	1¼ cups shelled fresh peas
8 (4-6-oz) quail	Chicken stock
½ cup butter	Salt and freshly ground pepper
About ½ cup brandy	½ lb prosciutto, cut into strips
½ onion, chopped	

Wash quail, pat dry and truss each with a skewer. Melt ¼ cup butter in a pan, put in quail and cook briskly for 15 minutes. Moisten with brandy and let this evaporate almost completely. Transfer quail to a serving dish with cooking juices, remove skewers and keep hot. In a separate pan, fry onion in remaining ¼ cup butter, add peas and a little stock, season with salt and pepper, cover and cook until tender. Just before removing peas from heat, add prosciutto. Garnish the quail with peas and prosciutto and serve.

Photograph page 172

INSALATA DI POLLO E RISO
Chicken and rice salad

PIEDMONT

Ingredients/serves 4	
1 cup cold cooked rice	Few tomatoes, sliced
$\frac{1}{2}$ cup sliced cooked chicken	Small lettuce leaves
$\frac{1}{2}$ cup diced cooked tongue	About 3 tablespoons vegetable oil
6 tablespoons slivered truffle (optional)	Juice of 1 lemon
1 tablespoon coarsely chopped fresh basil	3 tablespoons whipping cream
	Salt and pepper

Mix rice, chicken, tongue and truffle (if used) together in a bowl. Sprinkle with basil and decorate edges with tomatoes and lettuce. Make dressing by mixing together oil, lemon juice and cream; season with salt and pepper. Pour over salad.   *Photograph page 173*

POLLO FRITTO ALLA TOSCANA
Tuscan fried chicken

TUSCANY

Ingredients/serves 4	
1 (about $3\frac{1}{2}$ lb) broiler-fryer	Salt and pepper
1 large bunch parsley, chopped	Vegetable oil
Juice of 1 lemon	All-purpose flour
2-3 tablespoons olive oil	2 eggs, beaten

Cut the chicken into equal-sized pieces. Put into a casserole and sprinkle with parsley and lemon juice. Pour over olive oil and season with salt and pepper. Turn the chicken in the marinade and let stand for about 2 hours. Twenty minutes before you are ready to eat, heat some oil for frying in a large skillet. Remove the chicken from the marinade, dust with flour and coat with beaten egg. When the oil is very hot, add the chicken and fry over medium heat for about 15 minutes or until crisp and golden. Remove the chicken with a slotted spoon and drain on paper towels. Season again with salt and serve very hot.

QUAGLIE AL BRANDY ALLA ROMANA

QUAIL IN BRANDY WITH PEAS
For recipe, see p.170

INSALATA DI POLLO E RISO

CHICKEN AND RICE SALAD
For recipe, see p.171

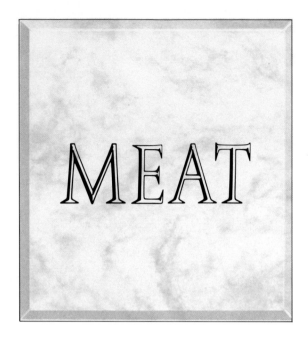

MEAT

Meat was a luxury in Italy until after the Second World War. The Italians are very fond of suckling pig, lamb and kid roasted on a spit over an open wood fire, but their favorite meat is probably veal. Some say that the word for veal — vitello — even gave the country its name.

ROGNONE DI VITELLO AL TEGAME CON FUNGHI

Veal kidneys with mushrooms

TUSCANY

Ingredients/serves 4	2 (½-lb) veal kidneys, fat and
1 tablespoon chopped onion	skin removed
1 clove garlic, crushed	¼ cup butter
Vegetable oil	Chopped parsley
4 fresh mushrooms, sliced	2 slices bread
Salt and pepper	

Fry onion and garlic in oil, add mushrooms, season with salt and pepper and cook through over medium heat. In another skillet, sauté kidneys in half the butter and a few tablespoons oil until done. Season, add mushroom mixture and cook briefly. Put on a serving dish, sprinkle with parsley and garnish with bread cut into triangles and fried in remaining butter and a little oil.

Photograph page 177

VITELLO CON PROSCIUTTO ALLA TOSCANA

Tuscan veal with ham

TUSCANY

Ingredients/serves 4	¼ lb prosciutto, cut into strips
1 (2-lb) veal rump roast	1 cup dry red wine
Salt and pepper	2 medium potatoes, boiled,
All-purpose flour	peeled, cut into chunks
3 tablespoons butter	1 clove garlic, crushed
Vegetable oil	Grated peel of 1 lemon
1 onion, chopped	Ground nutmeg

Season meat with salt and pepper and flour lightly. Melt butter in a heavy saucepan, add a little oil and brown meat. Stir in onion and prosciutto, pour in wine and cook over high heat until liquid is almost evaporated. Cover meat with water and continue to cook, turning meat occasionally. Just before veal is done, add potatoes and stir in garlic, lemon peel and nutmeg; let flavors mingle. Put meat on a serving dish, pour over cooking juices, surround with potatoes and serve.

Photograph page 177

ROGNONE DI VITELLO AL TEGAME CON FUNGHI

*V*EAL *KIDNEYS WITH MUSHROOMS*
For recipe, see p.175

VITELLO CON PROSCIUTTO ALLA TOSCANA

*T*USCAN *VEAL WITH HAM*
For recipe, see p.175

POLPETTE ALLA GENOVESE

Genoese meatballs

LIGURIA

Ingredients/serves 4	
1¾ cups ground cooked veal	2 tablespoons grated parmesan cheese
3 tablespoons fresh breadcrumbs, soaked in stock or milk and squeezed dry	Salt and pepper
	Ground nutmeg
1 clove garlic, crushed	1 egg, beaten
1 bunch parsley, chopped	All-purpose flour
Few fresh marjoram leaves	Vegetable oil
2 tablespoons dried mushrooms, soaked, drained, chopped	Solid vegetable shortening

In a bowl, mix the veal, breadcrumbs, garlic, parsley, marjoram, mushrooms and cheese. Season with salt, pepper and nutmeg; blend in egg, mixing well. Form mixture into balls, flatten slightly and dip in flour. Brown quickly in plenty of oil and shortening, then reduce heat and continue to fry until cooked through. Serve hot. *Photograph page 180*

COSTOLETTINE DI VITELLO ALLA VALDOSTANA

Veal cutlets with bacon and cheese

VENETO

Ingredients/serves 4	
4 veal cutlets	1-2 teaspoons finely chopped fresh rosemary
Salt	
	Brandy
1 egg, beaten	4 strips bacon, preferably smoked pancetta
Fresh breadcrumbs	
5 tablespoons butter	4 slices fontina cheese

Preheat oven to 400°F (200°C). Flatten cutlets slightly. Sprinkle with salt, dip in beaten egg and coat with breadcrumbs, pressing them on firmly. Heat butter in a pan until foamy and fry cutlets gently until cooked. Grease a large casserole dish, lay cutlets on bottom and sprinkle with finely chopped rosemary. Sprinkle on a few drops of brandy, then cover each cutlet with one strip of bacon and one slice of fontina. Bake for a few minutes or until cheese is partially melted. Serve very hot.

ROTOLO DI VITELLO RIPIENO
Stuffed shoulder of veal

LOMBARDY

Ingredients/serves 4	
I small onion, sliced	I bunch parsley, chopped
⅔ cup sliced sausage	I cup dry white wine
5 tablespoons butter	¼ cup grated parmesan cheese
¾ cup rice	1¾ lbs shoulder of veal in one piece
Salt and pepper	Rosemary sprig
5 cups boiling chicken stock	Vegetable oil

Preheat oven to 375°F (190°C). Fry onion and sausage in 2½ tablespoons butter. Add rice and season with salt and pepper; then cook, adding boiling stock gradually and stirring frequently. When rice is almost tender, add the parsley and ½ cup wine and leave the risotto on heat until wine is completely absorbed. Sprinkle on grated parmesan cheese. Flatten out veal, season and spread with risotto. Roll up meat, insert rosemary, secure with skewers and put in a pan with remaining 2½ tablespoons butter and a few tablespoons oil. Roast until brown, turning frequently. After 30 minutes, pour over remaining ½ cup wine and roast for I hour longer. Remove from oven, slice and serve immediately.

SALTIMBOCCA ALLA ROMANA
Veal scallops with ham

LAZIO, UMBRIA
AND
THE MARCHES

Ingredients/serves 4	
8 veal cutlets	8 fresh sage leaves
Salt and pepper	All-purpose flour
8 slices of prosciutto	5 tablespoons butter
	½ cup dry white wine

Flatten veal cutlets and sprinkle with salt and pepper. Cover each cutlet with a slice of prosciutto and a sage leaf, then fold each one in half and secure with a skewer. Flour lightly. Heat 4 tablespoons butter in a skillet and fry saltimbocca over medium-high heat until brown all over and cooked through. Remove with a slotted spoon and arrange on a serving dish. Add wine to cooking juices and reduce almost completely. Add remaining I tablespoon butter and stir until melted; pour hot sauce over saltimbocca. Serve at once.

Photograph page 180

POLPETTE ALLA GENOVESE

Genoese Meatballs
For recipe, see p.178

SALTIMBOCCA ALLA ROMANA

Veal Scallops with Ham
For recipe, see p.179

COSTOLETTE DI VITELLO ALLA PALERMITANO

Veal cutlets with pecorino

SICILY

Ingredients/serves 4	2 eggs, beaten
4 veal cutlets	5 tablespoons grated pecorino
Wine vinegar	cheese
Salt and pepper	Breadcrumbs
3 cloves garlic, crushed	Vegetable oil
I bunch parsley, chopped	

F latten cutlets slightly. Put on a plate, sprinkle on a little vinegar and let marinate for an hour or so. Drain, pat dry and season with salt and pepper. Mix garlic and parsley into beaten eggs; mix pecorino with breadcrumbs. Dip cutlets first into egg, then into breadcrumb mixture, pressing coating on firmly. Fry in hot oil until browned and crisp on both sides. Drain on paper towels and serve.

OSSIBUCHI ALLA MILANESE

Braised veal Milan-style

LOMBARDY

Ingredients/serves 4	I cup dry white wine
I small onion, sliced	Salt and pepper
¼ cup butter	About ⅓ cup chopped parsley
2 tablespoons olive oil	I clove garlic, chopped
All-purpose flour	Strip of lemon peel
About 4 lbs veal shanks, cut through bone into 2-inch pieces	

I n a large pan, cook onion in 2 tablespoons butter and the oil until softened. Lightly flour veal, place in pan and add wine. When wine has evaporated, season with salt and pepper and continue to cook gently, adding a little water or stock, if necessary, and not letting meat stick to bottom. Add parsley and garlic to ossobuco together with lemon peel when veal is half cooked. Continue cooking gently until meat is done. Heat a serving dish and arrange ossobuco on it, discarding lemon peel. Mix remaining 2 tablespoons butter into cooking sauce and pour over the ossobuco. Serve with saffron risotto.

ARROSTO DI MANZO ALLA CANNELLA
Pot-roast beef with cinnamon

Ingredients/serves 4	Salt and pepper
3 onions, thickly sliced	Pinch of ground cinnamon
6 tablespoons butter	Juice of 1 lemon
2 tablespoons vegetable oil	1 cup dry white wine
1 ¾ lbs boneless beef chuck roast	1 bay leaf

LAZIO, UMBRIA AND THE MARCHES

Put onions into a pan with butter and oil. Cook over low heat for 5 minutes. Add meat; sprinkle with salt, pepper and cinnamon. Pour in lemon juice and wine, add bay leaf, cover and cook over low heat for 2½ hours, turning meat every so often. When meat is tender, remove from pan, slice and arrange on a serving dish. Pour over the hot sauce from the pan and serve.

Photograph page 184

Radiccio

CARBONATA ALLA PIEMONTESE
Beef in red wine

Ingredients/serves 4	1 lb onions, sliced
⅓ cup solid vegetable shortening *or* butter	Salt and pepper
	1 cup condensed beef bouillon
1 ¾ lbs beef stew meat	Robust red wine

PIEDMONT

Preheat the oven to 375°F (190°C). Heat shortening or butter in a saucepan and brown meat in it. Remove with a slotted spoon and transfer to a plate. Then add the onions to pan and cook until very soft but not browned. (Add a little water if necessary.) When onions are very soft, arrange in a casserole and put meat on top. Season with salt and pepper and add bouillon. Then add just enough wine to cover. Bake until sauce is well reduced and meat is tender (about 1 hour) and serve with hot polenta.

ARROSTO DI MANZO ALLA CANNELLA

POT-ROAST BEEF WITH CINNAMON
For recipe, see p.183

SCALOPPINE DI BUE CON CAPPERI

BEEF TENDERLOIN WITH CAPERS
For recipe, see p. 186

SCALOPPINE DI BUE CON CAPPERI

Beef tenderloin with capers

LOMBARDY

Ingredients/serves 4	Vegetable oil
8 (4-oz) slices beef tenderloin	¼ cup capers
Salt and pepper	1 tablespoon chopped parsley
All-purpose flour	2-3 tablespoons vinegar *Balsamic*
5 tablespoons butter	Ground nutmeg

Pound beef slices lightly so all are the same shape. Sprinkle with salt and pepper; dust lightly with flour. Heat butter with a little oil in a pan. Brown meat; then add capers, parsley and 2 tablespoons cold water and cook, stirring frequently. In a separate pan heat vinegar with nutmeg over high heat, pour over meat and stir again. Serve meat on a platter, covered with sauce.

Photograph page 185

BISTECCHE DI MANZO ALLE ACCIUGHE

Steak with anchovies

**LAZIO, UMBRIA
AND
THE MARCHES**

Ingredients/serves 4	4 (4-oz) tender steaks
8 flat anchovy fillets	Salt
½ cup butter	½ cup pitted green olives
Pepper	

Press 4 anchovy fillets through a strainer and put in a bowl. Roll up remaining 4 anchovy fillets; set aside. Add ¼ cup butter and a pinch of pepper to strained anchovies and mix with a wooden spoon to a smooth paste. Shape mixture into a cylinder and wrap in foil. Refrigerate for 1 hour. Melt 1 tablespoon butter in a pan and add steaks. Cook over high heat for 2 minutes on each side. Drain, put on a dish, season with salt and pepper and keep warm. Add remaining 3 tablespoons butter to cooking juices, stir in olives and cook gently for 10 minutes, stirring occasionally. Take anchovy butter from refrigerator and cut into slices. Put a slice on each steak and top with a rolled anchovy. Garnish with olives, pour over hot sauce and serve.

Photograph page 189

BISTECCHE DI MANZO CON PROSCIUTTO E UOVA

Steak with ham and eggs

Ingredients/serves 4	Salt and pepper
6 tablespoons butter	4 slices prosciutto
4 (4-oz) tender steaks	4 eggs

EMILIA-
ROMAGNA

Melt 3 tablespoons butter in a pan and add steaks. Cook over high heat for 2 minutes on each side. Drain, season with salt and pepper and keep hot. Put remaining 3 tablespoons butter into pan and melt it. Add prosciutto and cook gently for 2 minutes. Break an egg onto each slice of prosciutto and cook until whites have set. Season eggs and lift out prosciutto with a spatula. Top steaks with prosciutto and eggs and pour over juices from pan. Serve at once.

BISTECCHE DI MANZO CON BURRO DI GORGONZOLA

Steak with gorgonzola butter

Ingredients/serves 4	1 tablespoon chopped parsley
6 tablespoons butter	Lemon juice
¼ cup crumbled mild gorgonzola cheese	4 (4-oz) tender steaks
	Salt and pepper

EMILIA-
ROMAGNA

Put 4 tablespoons butter, the gorgonzola, parsley and a few drops of lemon juice into a bowl and beat with a wooden spoon until mixture is smooth and creamy. Roll mixture into a cylinder and wrap in foil. Refrigerate for 1 hour. Melt remaining 2 tablespoons butter in a pan, add steaks and cook over high heat for 2 minutes on each side. Drain, season with salt and pepper and put on a serving dish. Cut gorgonzola butter into 12 slices and put 3 slices on each steak. Serve at once. *Photograph page 189*

BISTECCHE DI MANZO CON BURRO DE GORGONZOLA

STEAK WITH GORGONZOLA BUTTER
For recipe, see p.180

BISTECCHE DI MANZO ALLE ACCIUGHE

STEAK WITH ANCHOVIES
For recipe, see p.186

POLPETTONCINI ALLA NAPOLETANA FRITTI

Croquettes with mozzarella and lemon

CAMPANIA

Ingredients/serves 4	Salt and pepper
I lb lean ground beef	2 eggs, beaten
5 large slices stale bread, crusts trimmed, soaked in water and squeezed dry	I cup diced mozzarella cheese
	All-purpose flour
¼ cup chopped parsley	Vegetable oil
6 tablespoons grated parmesan cheese	Lemon wedges

C ombine beef, bread, parsley and parmesan in a bowl. Season with salt and pepper, then blend in eggs. Form into 4 croquettes and press mozzarella into them; re-shape croquettes. Roll in flour and fry in plenty of hot oil. Serve with lemon wedges. *Photograph page 200*

POLPETTONCINI ALLA NAPOLETANA CON POMODORO

Croquettes with mozzarella and tomato

CAMPANIA

Ingredients/serves 4	2 eggs, beaten
I lb lean ground beef	I cup diced mozzarella cheese
5 large slices stale bread, crusts trimmed, soaked in water and squeezed dry	All-purpose flour
	Vegetable oil
4 tablespoons chopped parsley	2 tablespoons chopped onion
6 tablespoons grated parmesan cheese	I lb tomatoes, peeled, seeded, pressed through a strainer
Salt and pepper	Coarsely chopped fresh basil

C ombine beef, bread, parsley and parmesan in a bowl. Season with salt and pepper, then blend in eggs. Form mixture into 4 oblong croquettes and press mozzarella into them; re-shape croquettes.Roll in flour and fry in plenty of hot oil. Meanwhile, fry onion in a pan with a few tablespoons oil, add tomatoes, season and cook over medium heat for about 20 minutes. Arrange croquettes in simmering sauce and leave to absorb flavors, scooping the sauce on top. Garnish with basil. *Photograph page 200*

SPIEDINI DI CARNE CON FUNGHI E PRUGNE

Beef kabobs with mushrooms and prunes

Ingredients/serves 4	8 bay leaves
16 prunes	Salt and pepper
About 1¼ lbs lean, boneless beef, cut in 12 equal cubes	1 teaspoon ground thyme
	Olive oil
12 mushroom caps	

LAZIO, UMBRIA AND THE MARCHES

Soak prunes in lukewarm water for 1 hour, then drain and pit. Preheat the oven to 425°F (220°C). Thread prunes, beef cubes and mushrooms alternately onto 4 metal skewers. Put a bay leaf at each end of each skewer. Season kabobs with salt, pepper and thyme and sprinkle with olive oil. Put in an oiled baking dish and bake for 10 minutes, turning and basting with cooking juices. Transfer to a serving dish and serve very hot.

AGNELLO ARROSTO CON SALSA DI FAVE

Roast lamb with lima bean sauce

Ingredients/serves 4	Rosemary sprig
1 cup cooked fresh lima beans	4 fresh sage leaves
2 cloves garlic	1 (2-lb) leg of lamb
½ cup grated parmesan cheese	Salt and pepper
About ½ cup olive oil	

TUSCANY

Preheat the oven to 375°F (190°C). Pound beans to a smooth paste with 1 clove of garlic, cheese and half the oil. Put other clove of garlic, rosemary, sage and remaining oil into an ovenproof casserole. Cook gently on top of the stove for 5 minutes, add lamb and brown on all sides. Season with salt and pepper, then roast for 1½ hours, turning and basting meat occasionally. When meat is done, transfer to a serving dish and keep warm. Put bean purée into juices in casserole, stir and heat through. Pour into a sauce boat and serve with the lamb. *Photograph page 193*

AGNELLO ARROSTO CON SALSA DI FAVE

ROAST LAMB WITH LIMA BEAN SAUCE
For recipe, see p.191

RAGÙ DI AGNELLO AI CARCIOFI

LAMB AND ARTICHOKE CASSEROLE
For recipe, see p.194

COSTOLETTINE DI AGNELLO CON FUNGHI

Lamb cutlets in mushroom sauce

LAZIO, UMBRIA AND THE MARCHES

Ingredients/serves 4	About ¹/₂ pint half-and-half (1 cup)
For the sauce	
¹/₂ small onion, chopped	Squeeze of lemon juice
¹/₄ cup butter	*For the lamb*
²/₃ cup fresh mushrooms, sliced	8 boneless lamb loin chops
Salt and pepper	¹/₂ cup butter
Ground nutmeg	Salt
Dry white wine	2 eggs, beaten
1¹/₂ cups condensed chicken stock	Breadcrumbs
1 tablespoon all-purpose flour	Parsley sprigs
2 egg yolks	

First make sauce. Fry onion in 2 tablespoons butter, add mushrooms, season with salt, pepper and nutmeg, moisten with a little white wine and cook, adding ³/₄ cup stock gradually. Melt remaining 2 tablespoons butter in a pan, mix in flour and gradually blend in ¹/₂ cup stock. Cook, stirring, until slightly thickened. Beat together egg yolks and remaining ¹/₄ cup stock; blend yolk mixture into mushroom mixture, then stir all into hot sauce. Blend in half-and-half and lemon juice. Adjust seasoning and stir over low heat until sauce has thickened. (Do not on any account allow it to boil.) Then cook the cutlets, browning them in ¹/₄ cup butter. Season with salt, remove from pan and allow to cool. Cover cutlets completely with egg and breadcrumbs. Heat remaining ¹/₄ cup butter in pan and brown breaded cutlets. Drain, garnish with parsley and serve with hot mushroom sauce.

RAGU DI AGNELLO AI CARCIOFI

Lamb and artichoke casserole

LAZIO, UMBRIA AND THE MARCHES

Ingredients/serves 4	Salt and pepper
1¹/₂ lbs lean boneless lamb (leg or shoulder), cubed	Chicken stock
	8 cooked artichoke hearts
¹/₂ cup butter	¹/₂ cup dry white wine
Vegetable oil	Chopped parsley

Brown meat in 5 tablespoons butter and a little oil, season with salt and pepper and cook over low heat until tender, adding stock as necessary. Cut artichoke hearts into strips and cook in remaining 3 tablespoons butter with a pinch of salt. Put lamb onto a dish, add wine to cooking juices and reduce. Pour onto lamb, garnish with artichokes, sprinkle with parsley and serve. *Photograph page 193*

AGNELLO IN AGRODOLCE ALLA SICILIANA
Sweet and sour lamb

Ingredients/serves 4	
1 (2 lb) lamb shoulder roast	Salt and pepper
2 cloves garlic	1 lb tomatoes, peeled, seeded, pressed through a strainer
Fresh rosemary leaves	1/2 cup wine vinegar
1/2 onion, sliced	4 teaspoons sugar
Vegetable oil	

SICILY

Wash lamb, pat dry and stick with slivers of garlic and leaves of rosemary. Fry onion in a heavy saucepan with a few spoonfuls of oil; then brown meat, season with salt and pepper and add tomatoes. Cover and cook for 45 minutes. Add vinegar and let some evaporate. Then add sugar and simmer for 45 minutes longer, adding a few spoonfuls of water or stock as necessary. Serve meat sliced and well covered with hot sauce.

SPIEDINI RUSTICI E RISO IN FORNO
Baked country kabobs with rice

Ingredients/serves 4	
1 lb lean, boneless pork (leg or shoulder)	Salt and pepper
	1/4 cup all-purpose flour
3 zucchini	Vegetable oil
1 cup fresh mushrooms	1 onion, chopped
2 firm tomatoes	1 cup dry white wine
3 bell peppers, seeded, cut into slices	1 1/4 cups rice

LAZIO, UMBRIA
AND
THE MARCHES

Cut pork into chunks. Cut zucchini, mushrooms and tomatoes into slices. Thread meat, zucchini, mushrooms, tomatoes and bell peppers alternately onto 4 wooden skewers. Sprinkle with salt and pepper; flour lightly. Heat some oil in an ovenproof casserole and lightly brown kabobs. Add onion and pour in 1/2 cup wine. Cover and cook for 10 minutes, without reducing sauce. Preheat oven to 400°F (205°C). Spoon rice around meat; add remaining 1/2 cup wine and enough water to cover. Bring to a boil. Cover and bake for 20 minutes. Let stand for 5 minutes before serving. *Photograph page 196*

BAKED COUNTRY KABOBS WITH RICE
For recipe, see p. 195

HAM SLICES WITH ANCHOVY SAUCE
For recipe, see p.199

COSCIOTTO DI MAIALE AL FORNO
Roast leg of pork

LAZIO, UMBRIA AND THE MARCHES

Ingredients/serves 4	1 tablespoon whole cloves
1 (about 3 lb) leg of pork	$\frac{1}{2}$ cup sugar
$\frac{1}{2}$ cup olive oil	3 cups dry white wine
Salt and pepper	$\frac{1}{4}$ cup vinegar
$\frac{3}{4}$ cup hot chicken stock	Cornstarch

S oak pork in cold water for 2 hours, then drain and pat dry. Preheat oven to 325°F (160°C). Pour oil into a large casserole. Season meat with salt and pepper and add to casserole. Roast for 3 hours, basting occasionally with a little hot stock. Drain leg over a plate and skim fat from drippings. Pour drippings out of pan and reserve. With a sharp knife, cut crosses into rind of pork leg; put a clove into each cross and sprinkle surface with sugar. Put leg back into roasting pan and return to the oven at 375°F (190°C) until sugar caramelizes. Mix wine with vinegar and reserved drippings and pour this mixture over meat. Cook for 1 hour longer. Transfer pork to serving dish. Skim fat from cooking juices, strain and bring to a boil. Thicken gravy with cornstarch. Pour it into a sauce boat and serve with leg of pork.

COSTOLETTE DI MAIALE ALLE OLIVE
Pork chops with olives

LAZIO, UMBRIA AND THE MARCHES

Ingredients/serves 4	Salt and pepper
20 cloves garlic	$\frac{3}{4}$ cup large green olives
4 pork chops	1 tablespoon solid vegetable
Vegetable oil	shortening
Vinegar	$\frac{1}{4}$ cup marsala *or* white wine
Rosemary sprig	$\frac{1}{4}$ cup condensed beef bouillon
Few fresh sage leaves	1 tablespoon chopped parsley

P eel 18 cloves of garlic; cook for 3 minutes in boiling water, then drain. Flatten chops and insert remaining garlic, cut into slivers. Prepare a marinade with oil, a little vinegar, rosemary, sage, salt and pepper. Put chops in marinade and let stand for 2 hours, turning occasionally. Drain and pat dry. Boil olives in water to cover for 10 minutes, remove from heat and keep hot in cooking liquid. Heat shortening in a pan with 1 tablespoon oil and add chops; brown for 3 minutes on each side. Reduce heat, add drained garlic and continue to cook for 12 minutes longer or until chops are cooked through, turning occasionally. Put chops on a plate and pile garlic and drained olives in the center. Pour marsala or wine into pan juices and reduce slightly; simmer for 5 minutes, then pour sauce onto the chops. Sprinkle with chopped parsley and serve.

Photograph page 200

PROSCIUTTO FRESCO DI MAIALE SALSATO

Ham slices with anchovy sauce

Ingredients/serves 4	1 small onion, chopped
8 (3-oz)slices ham	5 flat anchovy fillets, rinsed
Pepper	well, mashed
All-purpose flour	1 tablespoon capers, chopped
2 eggs, beaten	1 tablespoon chopped parsley
Few tablespoons fresh	Vinegar
breadcrumbs	Chicken stock
7 tablespoons butter	

EMILIA-ROMAGNA

F latten ham slices with a mallet and season with pepper; then dip in flour, egg and breadcrumbs. Melt 2 tablespoons butter in a pan, add onion and cook over low heat until soft. Add anchovy fillets, capers, parsley, 1 tablespoon flour and a little pepper. Stir over a high heat for a few minutes; stir in 2-3 tablespoons vinegar and let evaporate. Add enough stock to give a slightly thickened sauce. Dice 1 tablespoon butter and stir into sauce a piece at a time, making sure that each piece is fully incorporated before adding the next. Keep warm. In a separate pan, melt remaining 4 tablespoons butter; add breaded ham slices and brown on both sides, then reduce heat and cook for 10-12 minutes, turning occasionally. Arrange on a serving dish, pour over sauce and serve accompanied with buttered spinach.

Photograph page 197

POLPETTONCINI ALLA NAPOLETANA CON POMODORO
POLPETTONCINI ALLA NAPOLETANA FRITTI

CROQUETTES WITH MOZZARELLA AND TOMATO (TOP)
AND WITH MOZZARELLA AND LEMON (BOTTOM)
For recipes, see p.190

COSTOLETTE DI MAIALE ALLE OLIVE

PORK CHOPS WITH OLIVES
For recipe, see p.198

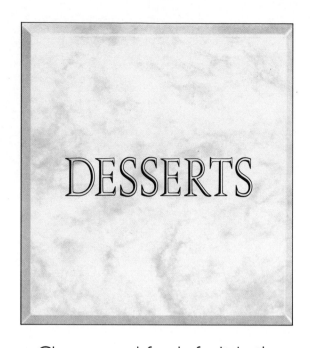

DESSERTS

Cheese and fresh fruit is the traditional Italian dessert for everyday, but on Sundays and special occasions lunch can be rounded off with elaborate concoctions of cream, chocolate and meringue on a sponge base soaked in liqueur. In addition to some of the sumptuous Italian desserts that can be made at home, this section also includes a selection of dessert cookies. These can be eaten in Italy at any time of the day — nibbled with coffee or an early morning glass of wine, or enjoyed after a heavy meal with a warming and syrupy liqueur.

FRAGOLINI FRITTI
Fried strawberries

LAZIO, UMBRIA
AND
THE MARCHES

Ingredients/serves 6	1 lb strawberries
½ cup all-purpose flour	5 tablespoons sugar
2 tablespoons butter, melted	About ¼ cup maraschino
1 egg	Vegetable oil for deep-frying
Milk	¼ cup powdered sugar
Brandy	

S ift flour into a bowl and mix in butter. Add egg and enough milk and brandy to make a smooth batter. Let stand for an hour. Trim and wash strawberries, then spread out on a plate. Sprinkle with the sugar and maraschino and let stand for about 30 minutes. Ten minutes before serving, beat egg white until stiff and fold into batter. Dip strawberries into the batter one by one, coating well, and deep-fry in plenty of oil until golden brown and crisp. Drain on paper towels. Put on a dish, sprinkle with powdered sugar and serve.

Photograph page 205

RAVIOLI DOLCI AL FORNO
Sweet baked ravioli

CAMPANIA

Ingredients/serves 6-8	For the filling
For the pasta	1½ cups whole unpeeled
3¾ cups all-purpose flour	chestnuts
⅔ cup butter	½ cup unsweetened cocoa
⅔ cup sugar	powder
4 eggs	¼ cup sugar
1 cake compressed yeast	½ cup chopped almonds
½ cup lukewarm milk (95°F, 35°C)	½ cup crushed amaretti cookies
	1 cup orange marmalade

F or the pasta, mix together flour with butter, sugar, 3 eggs and yeast dissolved in lukewarm milk. Knead dough for 20 minutes, cover and let rise in a warm place for an hour. *For the filling,* boil chestnuts, peel and press through a strainer or purée in a blender. Mix chestnut purée with cocoa, sugar, almonds, amaretti and marmalade. Preheat oven to 350°F (180°C). Roll out pasta into a thin sheet and cut into circles 2 inches in diameter. Place some filling on each; fold in half and press edges to seal. Arrange on a greased baking sheet. Beat remaining egg; brush over ravioli. Bake for 20 minutes.

Photograph page 205

FRAGOLINI FRITTI

*F*RIED *STRAWBERRIES*
For recipe, see p.203

RAVIOLI DOLCI AL FORNO

*S*WEET *BAKED RAVIOLI*
For recipe, see p.203

RISO DOLCE DI SAN GIUSEPPE ALLA TOSCANA

Sweet rice croquettes San Giuseppe

TUSCANY

Ingredients/serves 4	¼ cup seedless raisins, chopped
½ cup all-purpose flour	2 tablespoons pine nuts
2 cakes compressed yeast	I tablespoon superfine sugar
2½ cups lukewarm milk, (95°F, 35°C)	Grated peel of ½ lemon
	Vegetable oil
½ cup rice	Powdered sugar
I egg and 2 egg yolks	
Pinch of salt	

Mix 3 tablespoons flour with crumbled yeast and mix with enough lukewarm milk to form a dough. Knead into a ball and cut a cross on top. Put dough in a bowl and moisten top with milk. Cover and let rise in a warm place for 20-30 minutes or until doubled in bulk. Pour remaining milk into a pan, bring to boil, add rice and cook, uncovered, over medium heat until tender. Pour rice into a bowl and allow to cool, then add remaining 5 tablespoons flour, egg, egg yolks, salt, yeast dough, raisins, pine nuts, superfine sugar and lemon peel. Mix well, adding a few tablespoons milk, if necessary. Heat some oil in a skillet, shape rice mixture into balls and arrange in skillet (do not let croquettes touch each other). Fry until golden brown, drain on paper towels, dust with powdered sugar and serve. *Photograph page 208*

SFOGLIATELLE NAPOLETANE

Ricotta roll

CAMPANIA

Ingredients/serves 2-4	For the filling
For the pastry	1 egg and 3 egg yolks
2 cups all-purpose flour	$\frac{1}{2}$ cup superfine sugar
1 $\frac{1}{2}$ cups butter *or* margarine	1 tablespoon cornstarch
2 tablespoons sugar	1 $\frac{1}{4}$ cups hot milk
2 eggs	$\frac{1}{4}$ teaspoon vanilla extract
Pinch of salt	$\frac{1}{2}$ cup ricotta cheese
Milk	2 tablespoon diced candied orange peel
	1 egg, beaten (optional)
	Powdered sugar

Combine ingredients for pastry, adding enough milk to give dough a soft, elastic consistency. Knead well, cover and chill for 30 minutes. *For the filling,* beat 1 egg and 3 egg yolks with superfine sugar, add cornstarch and gradually mix in milk and vanilla. Pour into a pan; place over low heat and bring to a boil, stirring constantly. Remove from heat, allow to cool, and mix in ricotta and orange peel. Preheat oven to 375°F (190°C). Roll out pastry on a floured board, then cut into rectangles. Put filling on half the rectangles and cover with remaining rectangles, sealing edges firmly. Brush with beaten egg, if desired. Arrange on a greased, floured baking sheet and bake until golden brown. Dust with powdered sugar. *Photograph page 208*

POMPELMI E ARANCE IN INSALATA

Orange and grapefruit salad

CAMPANIA

Ingredients/serves 4	Superfine sugar
2 large oranges	Liqueur
3 large grapefruit	

Peel oranges and grapefruit and cut off all white membranes. Cut fruit crosswise into slices, then cut slices in half and arrange in a crystal bowl. Pour on juice left on the cutting board and sprinkle with plenty of sugar and your choice of liqueur. Chill for at least an hour before serving. *Photograph page 209*

SWEET RICE CROQUETTES SAN GIUSEPPE
For recipe, see p.206

SFOGLIATELLE NAPOLETANE

RICOTTA ROLL
For recipe, see p.207

POMPELMI E ARANCE IN INSALATA

*O*RANGE AND GRAPEFRUIT SALAD
For recipe, see p.207

TIMBALLO CON LE PERE ALLA PIEMONTESE

*T*IMBALE OF PEARS IN RED WINE
For recipe, see p.210

TIMBALLO CON LE PERE ALLA PIEMONTESE
Timbale of pears in red wine

PIEDMONT

Ingredients/serves 4	For the pastry
For the filling	1 cup all-purpose flour
1 lb pears, peeled, cored	⅔ cup superfine sugar
Red wine	½ cup yellow cornmeal
Sugar	⅔ cup butter
1 whole clove	Pinch of salt
Pinch of ground cinnamon	3 egg yolks

For the filling, cut pears into chunks and cook until tender in red wine with a little sugar and the spices. Remove clove; set pears aside. *For the pastry*, combine flour, sugar, cornmeal, butter (except for about 1 tablespoon), salt and egg yolks, adding a little water, if necessary. Cover and chill for about 1 hour. Preheat oven to 375°F (190°C). Roll out a little over half the pastry and line a tart pan; fill with pears. Dot with reserved butter. Roll out remaining pastry; make a lattice top and place on pears. Bake until golden brown.

Photograph page 209

ZABAIONE
Zabaglione

EMILIA-ROMAGNA

Ingredients/per person	1 heaping tablespoon sugar
1 egg, separated	2 tablespoons dry marsala

You can substitute dry white wine, Malaga or port for the marsala. If you use a liqueur, it is best to halve the quantity and add half dry white wine. Zabaione can be served with whipped cream or plain cookies, or it can be used to accompany other desserts. Put egg yolk into a small pan (copper, if possible) over medium heat. Add sugar and beat well with a whisk or wooden spoon. Gradually add marsala, stirring constantly; then either reduce heat or place pan over a larger pan of barely simmering water. Continue beating until mixture has risen and is light and fluffy. Make sure heat is not too high — if it is, you will feel the mixture begin to stick to pan bottom. If necessary, remove pan from the heat for a short time. To serve, pour into a dish and allow to cool — never leave it in the pan. If it is to be served cold, cover with waxed paper, pressing paper directly against surface of zabaione.

RICOTTA FRITTA ALLA ROMANA
Ricotta fritters

LAZIO, UMBRIA
AND
THE MARCHES

Ingredients/serves 4	
½ lb farmer's cheese	Vegetable oil
All-purpose flour	½ cup sugar
2 eggs, beaten	Pinch of ground cinnamon

Spread cheese on a flat plate to make a layer about 1 inch thick. Cut into 1″ x 2″ pieces; roll pieces in flour and chill for about 1 hour. Roll again in flour, then in beaten eggs. Fry in a wide pan with plenty of hot oil. When golden brown, drain, arrange on a serving dish and sprinkle with sugar mixed with cinnamon. Serve hot.

PANFORTE DI SIENA
Sienese spice cake

TUSCANY

Ingredients/serves 10-12	
1 tablespoon coriander seeds	¼ cup finely chopped walnuts
¼ cup unsweetened cocoa powder	⅔ cup coarsely chopped candied orange peel
2 tablespoons ground cinnamon	¼ cup coarsely chopped candied citron
1 whole nutmeg	2⅔ cups mixed candied fruit, coarsely chopped
3 cinnamon sticks	⅔ cup all-purpose flour
½ teaspoon whole cloves	Powdered sugar and a pinch of ground cinnamon (optional)
6 whole black peppercorns	
2½ cups blanched almonds	
½ cup honey	
1¼ cups superfine sugar	

First prepare two powders. Pound coriander in a mortar and mix half of it with cocoa and ground cinnamon. Grate nutmeg; grind together with cinnamon sticks, cloves, peppercorns and remaining coriander and set aside. Preheat oven to 350°F (180°C). Toast almonds until golden brown. Set aside. Put honey and superfine sugar in a copper pan over medium heat and stir constantly until syrup has reached the soft ball stage. Remove from heat; stir in almonds, walnuts, orange peel, citron, candied fruit, sifted flour and spice mixtures. Divide mixture into 2 portions; spread each portion on a greased baking sheet in a 1-inch-thick circle. Place a pie plate on each circle and cut around edges to make them even. Fasten a double thickness of foil around edges of each circle to keep it in shape on baking sheet. Bake for 30 minutes. Allow to cool before removing from baking sheet. Remove foil with scissors. Dust with powdered sugar mixed with cinnamon, if desired.

*S*ICILIAN *TRIFLE CAKE*
For recipe, see p.215

*S*LAVIC *FRUIT CAKE*
For recipe, see p.216

*G*ENOESE-STYLE SPONGE CAKE
For recipe, see p.218

*U*GLY BUT NICE!
For recipe, see p.219

ZUCCOTTO
Cream sponge deluxe

TUSCANY

Ingredients/serves 8-10	$\frac{1}{4}$ cup blanched almonds
6 eggs	6-8 tablespoons liqueur
$\frac{3}{4}$ cup superfine sugar	$3\frac{3}{4}$ cups whipping cream
Grated peel of 1 lemon	$\frac{1}{2}$ teaspoon vanilla extract
7 tablespoons all-purpose flour	$\frac{2}{3}$ cup powdered sugar
$\frac{1}{2}$ cup potato starch	Ground sweet chocolate
For the filling	Candied cherries (optional)
$\frac{1}{4}$ lb semisweet chocolate	
$\frac{1}{4}$ cup hazelnuts, toasted, skins rubbed off	

You can buy the chocolate decorations instead of making them. Prepare the cake the day before eating, as it will slice better. Grease and flour a deep 10-inch round baking pan. Preheat oven to 375°F (190°C). Using an electric mixer, beat eggs and superfine sugar together until very frothy. Then add lemon peel and sift in flour. Fold in potato starch. Turn into prepared pan and bake for 40 minutes. Cool on a rack. Melt chocolate over low heat. Pour some of chocolate into a pastry bag fitted with a fine writing tip. Pipe tiny circles of chocolate onto a sheet of waxed paper and let cool until set. Meanwhile, pour remaining chocolate onto another sheet of waxed paper, spread into a wide, thin sheet and let cool until set but not brittle; then cut into circles with a cookie cutter. Invert sheet with chocolate cutouts over another sheet of waxed paper, so that circles fall onto it; reserve chocolate trimmings. Finely chop hazelnuts and almonds; set aside. Cut 2 waxed paper strips and place in a 1$\frac{1}{2}$- to 2-quart mold to make dessert easier to unmold. Cut cake in half horizontally; cut each layer in pieces to fit bottom and sides of mold. Line mold with cake; moisten cake with 4-6 tablespoons liqueur of your choice. Melt reserved chocolate trimmings. Pour 2$\frac{1}{4}$ cups cream into a bowl and whip. Mix in tiny chocolate drops, almonds, hazelnuts, vanilla, $\frac{1}{2}$ cup powdered sugar and 2 tablespoons liqueur. Mix well, then pour half into mold and level off. Add melted chocolate to other half, and pour this too into mold. Cover with a waxed paper circle and push down the mixture with a piece of cardboard. Chill for 4 hours or more. Invert zuccotto onto a piece of waxed paper and remove paper strips. Dust with remaining powdered sugar. Then place 4 paper strips, each 1 inch wide, over the top of cake, crossing them and tucking edges underneath cake. Sift ground chocolate over spaces and carefully remove paper. Put two spatulas underneath cake and lift it onto a serving dish. Whip remaining 1$\frac{1}{2}$ cups cream and pipe rosettes of cream around and on top of zuccotto. Decorate with chocolate circles and candied cherries, if desired, and chill until ready to serve.

CASSATA ALLA SICILIANA
Sicilian trifle cake

SICILY

Ingredients/serves 8-10	For the topping
3 cups ricotta cheese	3 tablespoons apricot jam
.1 tablespoon pistachio nuts	1 tablespoon powdered sugar
$^2/_3$ cup semisweet chocolate pieces	1 $^1/_4$ cups superfine sugar
$^3/_4$ cup mixed candied fruit	1 tablespoon corn syrup
1 (9" × 5") loaf gingerbread	Orange flower water
1 lb superfine sugar	1 $^1/_4$ cups mixed candied fruit
Few drops vanilla extract	
Pinch of ground cinnamon	

L ine a 10-inch spring-form pan with waxed paper. Place ricotta in a bowl and beat until smooth. Blanch and peel pistachios and pound in a mortar. Chop the chocolate and candied fruit. Cut gingerbread into slices and line pan with it, reserving a few slices. Put 1 lb superfine sugar and a few tablespoons water in a pan; heat until sugar has dissolved. To ricotta, add dissolved cooled sugar, vanilla, cinnamon, chocolate, candied fruit and pistachios. Put this into pan, cover with remaining gingerbread slices and then another layer of waxed paper. Push down and chill for a few hours. Meanwhile make topping. Melt apricot jam, add powdered sugar and stir until dissolved. Remove pan sides and invert cassata onto a plate; remove waxed paper. Brush cassata with jam mixture. Over low heat, melt 1 $^1/_4$ cups superfine sugar and corn syrup, adding a few tablespoons of orange flower water. Stir well, then pour onto middle of cake and spread all over it with a spatula. Decorate cake with candied fruit and let topping set. Using 2 spatulas lift cake onto a serving dish. This classic topping for cassata is tinged with green from pounded pistachio nuts and decorated with candied peel.

Photograph page 212

POTIZZA ALLA FRUTTA SECCA

Slavic fruit cake

VENETO

Ingredients/serves 4	For the filling
For the pastry	³⁄₄ cup hazelnuts, toasted, skins rubbed off
2 cakes compressed yeast	
Salt	I cup chopped walnuts
¹⁄₂ cup sugar	¹⁄₂ cup golden raisins
I ¹⁄₄ cups lukewarm milk (95°F, 35°C)	¹⁄₂ cup rum
	¹⁄₂ cup butter
5¹⁄₄ cups self-rising flour	I cup superfine sugar
¹⁄₂ cup butter	4 eggs, separated
3 egg yolks	About ¹⁄₂ pint whipping cream (I cup), whipped
Grated peel of I lemon	
	Grated peel of I lemon
	Pinch of ground cinnamon
	I egg, beaten

F or the pastry, crumble yeast into a cup, add a pinch of salt, the sugar and lukewarm milk (reserving a few tablespoons). Put flour in a bowl, add yeast mixture and ¹⁄₄ cup butter and mix well together. Form dough into a ball and put into a floured bowl. Cut a cross on the surface, cover dough and let rise until doubled in bulk. Then add 3 egg yolks beaten with reserved milk, remaining ¹⁄₄ cup butter cut into pieces and grated lemon peel. Knead well, cover and let rise again. Then punch down, knead and let rise once more. *For the filling,* chop hazelnuts and mix with walnuts. Soak golden raisins in rum. Cream butter with ¹⁄₂ cup sugar. Beat 4 egg yolks with remaining ¹⁄₂ cup sugar until frothy. Add to butter-sugar mixture; fold in whipped cream, lemon peel and cinnamon. Add drained golden raisins and half the chopped nuts. Beat egg whites until stiff and fold in. Roll out dough on a floured board. Cut into 3 oblongs, the length of the baking sheet. Spread filling onto these; sprinkle with remaining nuts. Roll length-wise, brush with beaten egg and place on a greased baking sheet. Let rise for 15 minutes, then bake at 375°F (190°C) for an hour. *Photograph page 212*

STRUFFOLI ALLA PARTENOPEA

Honeyed Neapolitan doughnuts

Ingredients/serves 4	
1¼ cups all-purpose flour	1 tablespoon brandy
3 eggs	Salt
½ cups sugar	Milk
1½ tablespoons butter	Vegetable oil for deep frying
Grated orange and lemon peel	¾ cup honey
½ cup candied citrus peel, diced	Cake decorations

CAMPANIA

Mix flour with beaten eggs, 1 tablespoon sugar, butter, a little orange and lemon peel, 3 tablespoons candied citrus peel, brandy and a pinch of salt (add a little milk, if necessary). Shape dough into a ball, cover and let stand for an hour. Make thin sticks of dough and deep-fry in hot oil until golden brown. Drain on paper towels. Into a pan (copper, if possible) put honey, remaining 7 tablespoons sugar and a few tablespoons water. Bring to a gentle boil and simmer until syrup turns a yellow color. Reduce heat and add pastries, stirring all the while so that they are covered all over in honey. Remove with slotted spoon, put onto a wet dish, and mold with your hands into ring doughnut shapes. Sprinkle cake decorations over them and decorate with remaining 5 tablespoons candied peel cut into strips.

GENOISE
Genoan-style sponge cake

LIGURIA

Ingredients/serves 4	¼ teaspoon vanilla extract *or*
⅓ cup butter	grated peel of 1 lemon
4 eggs	1 tablespoon rum *or* cognac
½ cup superfine sugar	9 tablespoons all-purpose flour, sifted

G rease an 8-10-inch round cake pan and dust with flour. Cut butter up and heat until just melted in a small saucepan. Preheat oven to 350°F (175°C). Break eggs into a copper saucepan, add sugar and whisk until blended. Place pan over low heat or over a larger pan of barely simmering water; whisk until egg mixture is warm to the touch. Remove from heat and continue whisking until mixture has cooled. Add vanilla or grated lemon peel, rum or cognac, and flour. Mix well, then add the melted butter gradually, not letting it stick to the bottom. Put mixture into cake pan — it should come a little more than halfway up sides — and bake for about 30 minutes or until center springs back when touched. Turn out onto a rack to cool. If you want to fill genoise, prepare it a few days ahead of time, wrapping it in waxed paper. *Photograph page 213*

STRACA-DENT ALLA ROMAGNOLA
Munchies

EMILIA-
ROMAGNA

Ingredients/makes 8	¾ cup superfine sugar
1½ cups blanched almonds	3 egg whites, lightly beaten
¾ cup all-purpose flour, sifted	

P reheat oven to 350°F (175°C). Chop almonds. Mix flour, almonds, sugar and beaten egg whites and knead with your hands until you have a smooth mixture. Grease a baking sheet and heap mixture on it in small mounds. Bake until golden brown. Allow to cool completely and arrange on a pretty plate, then serve.

AMARETTI
Almond cookies

Makes 30 cookies	Pinch of baking powder
1¼ cups blanched almonds	4 egg whites
1¼ cups superfine sugar	¼ to ½ teaspoon almond extract

CAMPANIA

Preheat oven to 275°F (135°C). Butter a baking sheet and flour it. Put almonds and a little sugar in a mortar and pound to a powder. Pour powder into a bowl with remaining sugar and baking powder and stir. Beat egg whites until stiff; fold in almond mixture, then almond extract. Spoon into a pastry bag. Pipe mixture onto baking sheet, making small mounds. Bake until well dried out (about 40 minutes) and let cool before serving.

BRUTTI MA BUONI
Ugly but nice!

Makes 50 cookies	1 cup powdered sugar
1 cup blanched almonds	Ground cinnamon
3 egg whites	Ground cloves
¼ teaspoon vanilla extract	

VENETO

Preheat oven to 300°F (150°C). Chop almonds finely. Beat egg whites in a bowl until stiff, then fold in chopped almonds, vanilla and sugar; add cinnamon and cloves to taste. Put walnut-sized pieces of mixture onto a greased and floured baking sheet, spacing cookies well apart. Bake for 40 minutes. Put on rack to cool and store in an airtight container.

Photograph page 213

INDEX

Page numbers in *italics* refer to
the illustrations

Acknowledgements

The publishers gratefully acknowledge the kind assistance of the following: Gruppo Editoriale Fabbri, Milan, and, in particular, Virginia Prina for her helpfulness throughout the production of this book; Linda Sonntag for writing all introductory text and for her help at every editorial stage; Anna Nyburg for her translating skills; John Heseltine for additional photography; and Barbara Croxford.

Picture credits

All photographs except the following were supplied by Gruppo Editoriale Fabbri, Milan, and remain their copyright: pages 3, 11, 15, 18, 21, 28 (top), 31-3, 36-7, 40-4, 47, 50, 61 (bottom), and the background shots on pages 66-7, 88-9, 104-5, 122-3, 176-7 and 196-7 © Quarto Publishing Limited.

Guide to uncaptioned photographs

Pp. 66-7, Florence; *p. 70*, Venice; *pp. 74-5*, Venice; *pp. 78-9*, Apucali, Lombardy; *pp. 84-5*, Florence; *pp. 88-9*, looking north-east from Castello di Cacchiano; *pp. 92-3*, Umbria; *pp. 100-1*, Ancona, the Marches; *pp. 104-5*, Florence; *pp. 108-9*, San Miniato, near Pisa; *pp. 114-5*, Celle di Macra, near Cuneo, Piedmont; *pp. 118-9*, Lombardy; *pp. 122-3*, San Gimignano, Tuscany; *pp. 126-7*, Rome; *pp. 134-5*, Amalfi; *pp. 138-9*, Castel Gardena; *pp. 142-3*, Padua; *pp. 148-9*, Emilia-Romagna; *pp. 152-3*, the Appenines, between Riolo and Brisighellia; *pp. 156-7*, Rieti, Umbria; *pp. 160-1*, Valcamonica, near Lake Garda, Lombardy; *pp. 164-5*, Bologna, Emilia-Romagna; *pp. 168-9*, Rome; *pp. 172-3*, Bari; *pp. 176-7*, Sorrento; *pp. 180-1*, Sicily; *pp. 184-5*, Bolzano; *pp. 188-9*, Grado, Friuli; *pp. 192-3*, Siena; *pp. 196-7*, the Tuscan countryside around San Gimignano; *pp. 200-1*, Cilento; *pp. 204-5*, Molise; *pp. 208-9*, Valle d'Aosta, Piedmont.